Return to Mother
Returning Home

Reflections on the
End of My Mother's Life

Ruth R. Williams, LCSW

Return to Mother, Returning Home

Reflections on the End of My Mother's Life

Copyright © 2015

Ruth R. Williams, LCSW

Cover photo by Ruth R. Williams

Cover design by Ron Ault

ISBN 978-1514149188

I would like to dedicate this book to hospices all over the world, whose wonderful staff (all divinely commissioned in my best estimation!) gently and gracefully accompany folks during their intimate time of transition from this world to the next . . .

. . . and to all the angels—in that other world and in this one— who helped us as a family during that precious and sacred time. I thank you.

Table of Contents

Return to Mother, Returning Home

Reflections on the End of My Mother's Life

Introduction

Herewith my own disclaimer:

I realize that everything I say in this book is about my own personal experience. No one else had it, nor can anyone else interpret it. It's simply and profoundly that—my experience, filtered through my own perception. My own. My experiences are just that—my experiences. Even when others were present, I was in my own skin, with my own thoughts, feeling my own private emotions, feeling my own sense of presence of Spirit.

I seek to share these experiences as an offering of sorts, demonstrating that the path that awaits each one of us is oh-so-personal. And that those of us who are observers, cheerleaders, mourners, midwives of the dying, or reluctant bystanders each have our own unique way of being in such intimate surroundings, on such sacred ground.

My own family members were often with me. Hospice folks and nursing home folks were at times present. We may have been in the same room at the same time with the same exact "characters" visible (who knows who may have been "invisibly" with us!). However, our experience in that space and time was and is our own.

So, I'll apologize now—at the beginning of my sharing—and get that out of the way, just in case I inadvertently mischaracterize someone or say something that someone else *knows* is inaccurate! I'm not sure what, specifically, I'm apologizing for, but I am, just in case! Like it or not, sharing experiences in such a tender and often emotionally fragile time can bring out differences among individuals (even those closest to us). And recording, reporting, and recounting experiences can be full of "errors," so to speak. I make no claims that this is a historical document; instead, this is my own view, my own perspective, through my own eyes and heart.

All that is seen, heard, felt, and known is in divine perfection, because we all are divine creations! And, in the presence of someone on the brink of that next mysterious adventure, the divine is surely present.

Whether the dying person is a friend or relative, patient or resident . . . child, parent, spouse, or partner, with their own unique diagnosis, their own one-of-a-kind journey, we silently recognize that they/we are not alone. Even if we recognize the presence of Other/God/Creator/Spirit/the Holy at no other time, we do now—because, in these precious moments, it's difficult to ignore.

Another silent presence is our own death, our own finite nature. That is a "presence" we rarely speak of—but it is very real, and its true proximity is usually unknown.

And that ties it all together. That ties *us* all together.

Strangely (to me, at least), we seem to be able to pretend we are not One. But in that moment, the invisible, often palpable energy of together-ness—One-ness—can supersede all else. For we all step across that line when our inevitable time comes. Some may leap, others may dip one tentative toe into the eternal waters, but we all travel onward when "our time" arrives.

It is so.

My own precious mother invited me to be a part of her journey. In her own surprising way, she called to me and I answered that call. And because of my own passion for the work of hospice and my compassion for the dying (and the living), I'm sharing my own story.

In my work as a grief counselor, people often preface their stories with, "You may think I'm crazy." Once they realize I will *not* think they're "crazy," they are eager to share dreams, visions, experiences of touch, even photographs. Life after death still remains a mystery, although people who share "near death experiences" often have similar observations to report.

My mother's diagnosis at the end of her life was "failure to thrive." I often think another way to put that might be, from the "patient's" perspective, "I'm done! Let me out of here!" But there's no medical code for that. And so it is . . .

* * * * * * * * * * * * * * * *

Note: The indented and italicized sections are "reflections" of a different variety, detours from the diary-like recounting of my time with Mother. It's truly the way my mind works; I hope you'll be able to follow along!

Chapter 1: Mother Is Lost Somewhere in "Dementia-land"

On Christmas of 2008, we met as a family for our holiday celebration at the nursing home. Our sweet mother had been living there for some three years at that point. This was our third Christmas together with her in the nursing home.

This year, there were subtle changes. That's part of the devastation of dementia. It can indeed be subtle in a very cruel way; the person you know slips away incrementally, much like a fog that's dense at spots, then clears away, then returns . . .

I, being the out-of-town daughter, had trouble noticing significant differences. So I know my in-town sisters may not have noticed dramatic changes either.

This Christmas, Mother didn't speak at all. She'd been in a wheelchair for about a year. Her brain was no longer able to tell her legs what to do. She had to be fed. Our tradition for those three years at the nursing home was to bring in fast-food fried chicken. Mother's eyes were vacant for much of the time. One special moment was when her one and only son, my brother (the youngest), was sitting next to her. We'd been there for quite a while when, all of a sudden, there was a look of recognition—as if she were saying, "I know you! I know you!" It was magical, but it didn't last. We're genetically wired for taking pictures, so I have a great shot of my brother and mother at that very moment. However, in another photo from that day, Mother has those vacant eyes again, and yet another could be captioned, "Who are these people?"

She had moments of being present, when she'd respond to physical touch. My brother-in-law has a special touch which she seemed to recognize. And, when I put my hands on her shoulders, she responded much like a kitten, begging for more. I rubbed her back as she almost purred with delight. Still no words.

As our time was coming to an end, I stood behind her, placing my cheek next to hers, and whispered, "When you're ready to leave, come visit me in my dreams." No response. I have been an avid dreamer for many, many years, choosing to journal my nighttime dreams for just as many. I thought I was suggesting that she come visit me in my dreams, once she became spirit.

That day, she did speak one word. As I was wheeling her back to her room, she could see lots of holiday decorations. I heard her quietly say, "Christmas." Sweet.

Chapter 2: My Own Dreaming History

Mother was aware of my vivid dreaming. I've been recording my dreams off and on since the '70s, and I'd occasionally describe a fascinating one to her by phone. I've had some pretty amazing dreams through the years. Sometimes they help me process what's been going on in my daytime world. Sometimes they give me new ways of looking at my life, at my relationships, at my experiences. Sometimes they give me information about people who are in my life. And sometimes they even seem to give me a little bit of information about what's to come . . .

Earlier that year, in September 2008, I'd had a dream of my father, who died in 1983, a full 25 years previously.

The first image in the dream was of a staircase. I rode my bicycle to the staircase and parked it at the bottom of the stairs (I believe I did that so I'd be able to return). The stairs were colorful, vibrant. As I climbed the spiral staircase, what I observed around me were lively "creatures"—almost elf-like. It was a happy place, but very "other-worldly." There was even someone checking our bags, almost like in a concert venue, making sure no one was hiding a camera! As I came to the top, I realized I did have a camera in my bag—oops! My father was at the top, waiting for me. He was healthy, younger than I now remember him, but he was clearly my father. He did not speak a word, but seemed to want me to take his picture (he enjoyed photography when he was alive) to share with others, to share that he was all right. The distinct difference was that he seemed "whole," which was different from his earthly self. He was not a happy person in human form, but in his heavenly form, he finally seemed content.

As I went back down the stairs, there sat my mother in her wheelchair. She was most definitely her human self—not speaking, but making unintelligible utterings. Standing beside her was my younger sister, who was helping her pack her bag, getting her ready for her journey.

When I awoke, I believed I was being sent the message that Mother was preparing for her next step—the death of her physical body.

For those who are tiptoeing into another world during the daylight hours, it may not be at all unusual to reach out to others during the sleeping hours. As I came to learn in the weeks and months to follow, the subconscious mind, dreamtime, and inexplicable connections "in Spirit" between human beings—all were and are part of Life. All of those intangible, indescribable, inexplicable phenomena have the ability to touch us at the depths of our soul, our spirit, if we allow it.

Chapter 3: Mother Enters the Care of Hospice

In early 2009, the sign of Mother's decline that warranted hospice care was weight loss. During her first years in the nursing home, she'd gained weight consistently. In our family, food was always a priority—and a passion! So, take away the parts of the brain that govern discernment about how much food is sufficient, as well as the ability to burn calories, and weight increases. When Mother began to lose weight, it was a definite decline. When she began to lose weight more rapidly, hospice was called in.

Since I work for a hospice as a grief counselor, I have a definite understanding of what a blessing hospice employees can be. In my office, I have a bookmark tacked above my desk that says, "Hospice employees are not hired, they're called." I believe it. It seems to be more of a mission than a job to most employees.

How hospice works in a facility like a nursing home, though, was new to me. I have more of a connection with home care teams than facility teams. However, when my older sister shared that she was meeting with the hospice folks, I was all in favor of it. And they were/are great.

One day in April 2009, on the way to work (about a 30-minute commute), I spontaneously was overwhelmed with grief. My heart was hurting. I began to sob, yet my consciousness was aware of nothing out of the ordinary. Where was this coming from? My first thought was of the closest two people in my life—my daughter and husband. So I called them both. Fortunately, they each answered my phone call. Both were safe. My husband asked, "What about your mother?" That was a possibility, of course. I had spoken to my younger sister that morning. The oldest sister, the first-born, who did most of the practical stuff with Mother, was actually out-of-state, but I'd spoken to her the previous evening. And my intuitive self (which I trust more and more these days!) said my brother was fine as well.

So—Mother! I'd call Mother next! I'd not even tried to call Mother since she'd been in the nursing home. Both sisters were there in town with her, so any conversations we attempted to have with Mother were always coordinated by them. Luckily, I had the telephone number of the nursing home in my phone, so I called there (this was all still on the way to work!). I explained that I'd never done this before, so I wasn't sure how to ask for her since she didn't speak. They transferred me to her floor, to the nurses' station. It was a while before they connected me to someone who could talk with me about Mother. When they did, the nurse asked me if my sister had called me (she was visiting Florida but was still the "go to" gal for emergencies). Nope. She hadn't. Then the nurse said, "It's strange you should call right now. I just talked with your sister. Your mother fell this morning. I'm sitting with her. She's behaving normally. She seems to be all right, but we felt we should at least inform a family member." Wow!

And that's when the "Mother link" was established. Strange. And wonderful. And cosmically cool. But very unexpected.

You see, Mother and I had never been exceptionally close. Nothing really negative, but no bond that would create such a reaction, or at least none that I was aware of! So I was a bit surprised by this unusual "cosmic/telepathic" connection. And little did I know what was still to come.

Chapter 4: Our Relationship and Mother's First Call for Help

Mother had been a definite influence in my years at home. I went away to college just a few months after turning 17. I was ready to be out of our crazy household. There were lots of gifts growing up in our home, but also lots of challenges. When I was ready to leave, I was ready to leave. And I enjoyed the fact that, other than summers at home, I was moving away from the day-to-day influence of my parents.

Mother was a home economist by training, not by employment. She shared her wisdom with me. Of the three girls, I was the one who most wanted to learn all about sewing and cooking. I made most of my school clothes (dresses, of course, back in those days!). And Mother was also very creative in her culinary adventures, which was helpful since our budget was usually limited. Sardine pizzas were a favorite—well, maybe not a favorite, but at least quite a conversation piece!

The other thing that stood out in our relationship was correspondence. Since I was the gal who left home, we were pen pals. She was wonderful about keeping in touch. I always enjoyed seeing what articles she'd tear out of the newspaper to send me, what tidbits about life she'd convey through her letters. She kept this up for years—it was delightful. I kept most of her letters, and in later years, I learned she kept many of mine.

We also shared a deep spirituality. She was the one who showed us a faith-based life. She did her best to keep us grounded in some type of religion and spirituality despite a very emotionally challenging household (as I shared, my father was not a happy person, which was difficult for us all).

Reflecting on all that has happened since that April day, I believe there are many reasons I was selected to accompany Mother on this journey toward her physical death. One of the reasons may be that she knew I believed that dreams can be a connection to a Higher Consciousness, the "Great Cosmic Soup," so to speak. I, like Carl Jung, believe in something he called the collective unconscious, to which we can all have access if we so choose and if we learn to plug in. One of the ways I believe I plug in is through my dreams.

She also knew I believe in hands-on healing and that we can be conduits for God to others. One very tender memory I have of Mother is from around 1995, when she was 73. A dear neighbor of mine was dying in the care of hospice. Months earlier, I'd had my first training in Healing Touch, an energetic healing modality. There is a technique to assist in transition from this life to the next. I asked my neighbor if I had her permission to offer Healing Touch to her husband, my friend. I also quietly asked permission of her husband, on some amazing level, soul to soul. She agreed, as I believe he did. And so I began.

My mother was in town visiting, so she was at the neighbors' home with me to share this very intimate time with them. When I completed the process, I went and sat with Mother. We snuggled close, head to shoulder, and she warmly said, "I believe this is the closest I've ever felt to you." A sacred moment.

That April day, when I believe Mother let me know she was hurting, I believe she also was opening up the lines of communication. Somehow I knew that she would let me know when I should go be with her, perhaps to help her die, to assist in her transition from this world to the next. *Okay, Mother, just let me know.*

In early May, my oldest sister was still away. My younger sister took the initiative to visit the nursing home and called me—on Mother's Day—hoping to connect us at least via phone. Happily, it worked! She put Mother on the speaker phone, and when I said, "This is Ruth," she let out an "Ahhh!" I said a few words, and when I signed off, saying, "I love you, Mother," she replied with something that sounded very, very close to "Love you." Tears come to my eyes even now, just remembering.

My younger sister was the one who seemed closest to Mother emotionally (aren't family dynamics fun?!). They would "hang out" with one another, spending time together like girlfriends. Since I had lived away for 35 years, Mother and I didn't get the chance to do that very often. But she and Mother were very attached in their own wonderful way.

One intriguing piece of this story is that my sister had taken some wonderful steps in her life. She had graduated from college, bought her first home, settled into a new job, and was overall doing well.

Who knows what's involved in a soul's decision to leave planet Earth and head heavenward? What pieces—body/mind/spirit—have to come together to take flight? In

Mother's case, she didn't have any particular physiological ailment or disease that would cause her body to stop.

One of the gifts of being a grief counselor is hearing the heartwarming stories of clients. Several have shared that their loved ones speak of wanting to "go home." While our first instinct may be to presume they mean an "earthly home," it often becomes clear that they are referring to their "heavenly Home" (and that "Home" I feel compelled to capitalize, somehow elevating it as "it" so well deserves!). Perhaps the closer they get to their heavenly Home, the more it begins to feel like home.

An observation I have made through my years in practice as a psychotherapist and specializing now as a grief counselor, is that it seems—as someone gets closer and closer to the point of stepping into that next realm—that some amount of choice seems to be available. Whether the diagnosis is cancer or dementia or end stage renal disease or anything else terminal, when the endpoint is within reach, the patient seems able (in many or maybe even most cases) to "choose" when that will happen (notice I didn't say "always"!). Whether it's lingering much longer than anticipated or leaving more quickly than expected, when the family looks back, it's often observed that there may have been a person or event to wait for, a moment of privacy desired, a particular hand to hold, or even another's final departure to await. Life and death. Intriguing. Sacred.

The best way I could describe to people what happened starting at the end of April was that my "heart light" was turned on, much like in the movie *E.T.* In the movie, the little extraterrestrial character had a heart-like internal organ which began to glow when it received a signal from the mother-ship! It was as if I were being called home. I started dreaming . . .

Chapter 5: Mother Calls Me Home

As June approached, the call from my "Mother ship" kept getting stronger and stronger. My younger sister was trying to arrange a meeting of the siblings to help her with some home improvement tasks. I was trying to arrange a "vacation" home (with the underlying purpose of possibly helping Mother "transition," i.e., die). So, we coordinated it all. I went early, visited some friends, and had lots of walks down memory lane. I was walking down Mother's memory lane as well, visiting a home where both of us had lived as college students! Her four single aunts all shared a house. They were all living when she stayed with them. Two had died and two were in a nursing home when I lived there my last year of college. On a lovely spring day, I got up the courage to knock on the door of the house the four aunts had shared. The gracious homeowner showed me around. It was delightful—the floor even creaked in the same places it had some 35 years earlier!

Even before seeing Mother for the first time on that visit, I met with some of the hospice staff. I'd spoken with them on the phone, but this gave me the opportunity to meet them face to face. The chaplain and the social worker met me at their office. I "confessed" to them that I had an ulterior motive—that I believed Mother had "called" me (through my dreams) to come help her die. Being in hospice, they had heard many stories, so they didn't (at least not to me!) discount the possibility that Mother was indeed asking for help to get out of a very difficult—or at least minimal—existence. And, in a delightful way, I felt as if we were almost in the same "club," so to speak. We were in the business of death and dying and grief. So I didn't feel any hesitation in sharing what was in my heart and on my mind that day. And they truly did seem to understand.

I've learned in working in the hospice community (it does feel more like a community than a "regular" job) that there is a delightful sense of acceptance of the vast range of human experience in that journey toward death. I felt this acceptance with those lovely folks as well.

I went to visit Mother next. She was in her room. I honestly don't remember much of that brief visit. She wasn't very present that day.

The visit I will treasure in my heart always was on a Thursday. They still were taking her to the dining hall at that point, but she required a "feeder" since she was not usually able (i.e., mentally and physically "present") to feed herself. When I arrived, she was sitting alone, bib around her neck, plate beside her. She seemed very absent, but I tried for some recognition. Not much. I wheeled her back to her room, and at some point, she began to recognize me. As she awakened to my presence, I held her hand, speaking softly to her. She gradually became more and more present with me. I could see it in her eyes. Now, reflecting back on those amazing last days with her, I believe she was literally coming back into this world from the other world she seemed to be visiting more and more often.

What brought me to tears was that she reached out to stroke my cheek. Her right hand was contracted and not very useful. However, with her left hand and her very limited strength, she reached out, as our eyes connected, to stroke my cheek. In that moment, the love felt so overwhelmingly deep and profound, it defies description. It was a heart to heart connection that stretched beyond space and time. Very present. Very deep. Very eternal. Very sacred. *I love you, Mother.*

Time did stand still. And when I got up to say goodbye, she had already left again, going to some other place and perhaps some other time. I felt as if this truly might be our goodbye.

And what a lovely, heartfelt goodbye it truly was.

Chapter 6: Mother Makes Her First Attempt to Exit

When I went to the nursing home the next morning, I planned to meet the hospice nurse face to face for the first time. (She wasn't able to be there when I met the social worker and chaplain.) I called her when I drove into the parking lot, and she agreed to meet me in Mother's room shortly. When I arrived in Mother's room, she was non-responsive. I decided to do the Healing Touch technique for transition, just like I had done years earlier with our neighbor. Perhaps yesterday, Mother truly was letting me know she was ready, and we really had said our goodbyes.

I began to observe her breathing. It was what I call "intermittent breathing," but the hospice nurses sometimes use the term "Cheyne-Stoking"—heavy breathing followed by long pauses. I began to count breaths and estimate the space in between them.

Mother, being the home economics queen, even had a method for counting seconds (for things like beating egg whites or holding an iron over a mending patch). She'd say, "One chimpanzee, two chimpanzee . . ." So, of course, in your honor, Mother: "One chimpanzee, two chimpanzee."

The pauses seemed to lengthen. Should I call the hospice nurse? No, she was on her way.

When she arrived, I shared that Mother had been like this for a while. Since I was not a medical person, I obviously didn't officially know anything! So her observations were welcome and not at all surprising. She pointed out that, indeed, the breaks Mother was taking from breathing were getting longer and longer. She felt her hands and feet, and even placed my hands on her feet, showing me that they were beginning to cool down. The nurse announced, "I believe this is her day. Let's call your sisters."

By this time the social worker and even the hospice aide had arrived as well. She wanted to give Mother a little clean-up for her special day. She did so in an amazingly tender and loving way. Mother, we believe, saw her own mother's image in the hospice aide. In old pictures of Mother's own mother, when she was younger, there was an amazing resemblance. Mother could be a bit fussy at times; however, she always seemed to accept this gal's touch. The nurse reminded me of Mother's sister-in-law, who may have been the closest thing Mother ever had to a sister (she was an only child). I asked about calling my brother, since he and my husband were planning to come later on anyway (remember, the fix-it team was already scheduled to help my younger sister at her house). The nurse asked, "How far does he have to come?" I said he'd be there in about four hours if he started right now. She said, "I don't think he'll make it. Your mother could be gone in an hour."

My sisters were together, only a few minutes away, so they arrived almost instantly. We all shed some tears and called our brother, sharing what the hospice nurse was telling us. He said he would do his best to get on the road as quickly as possible. My husband began his journey to join us as well.

Meanwhile, the nursing home chaplain came by, as did two hospice chaplains. Even her local church pastor came by; there was a string of some four clergy over the next few hours. We're a musical family, so one of the chaplains brought some hymnals and we sang, harmonizing and sometimes choking back tears. Scriptures were read, prayers were said. It was all very lovely and very moving.

She continued to breathe, not actively responding to anyone and yet hanging on. The primary thought we all had was that she was waiting for the missing child, her one and only son, to arrive. The social worker leaned in to her ear, telling Mother the girls were here and her son was on the way.

Mother began perking up. She decided to stay! After all, we were throwing her a big party. She'd be silly not to stay for her own celebration! When we began to realize this indeed had been a false alarm, my older sister asked Mother, "Would you like some ice cream?" She gingerly spoke an entire sentence: "I would love some!"

She's back!

Later on, in the midst of trying to decide what to do next (now that she'd decided to hang around a little longer), I leaned over to give her a kiss. She puckered up for one of her on-the-lips kisses! Our brother, who by this time had arrived, had taught her that. So I called out to the hallway, where the others were gathered, saying, "Mother's giving out kisses—better come and get one!" So they all came in to receive their precious kisses. My, oh my—what a day!

My younger sister was going to stay that night, but since her house was the intended "project" for the weekend (before Mother decided she was exiting), she eventually went home when it was clear Mother had changed her mind and would hang out a little longer. I decided I would "keep watch" or "hold vigil" as the hospice folks termed it. It was all perfect. The others kept very busy, crossing everything off the list in the home repair venture. They accomplished so much they had to start on another list! A very successful weekend, all in all. I pride myself on efficiency (at times); consequently, I had taken plenty of things to work on while I was waiting and sitting with our dear mother. Nevertheless, I found myself choosing to be present with her, intermittently doing some Healing Touch, but mostly just "being" with her. It was nice.

She started doing an interesting motion that I found fascinating. She would hold on to the bedrail and seemingly pull herself to it, almost as if she were exercising. In her younger days, she was a good example for us youngsters. She would watch Jack LaLanne on television and follow his calisthenics, using everyday equipment like a simple chair. Had she perhaps decided that, since she hadn't died quite yet, she should be "working out" and keeping herself strong enough to postpone the inevitable just a little longer? Maybe so!

In fact, when it came time for us to leave, I hesitated a little, knowing that I could probably extend my time off a little more. But when I went by one last time to say goodbye and saw her "exercising" again, I decided she wasn't quite ready to let go. I truly believe she had planned to make her exit; however, since we decided to celebrate with her, she decided to delay it a little longer.

Chapter 7: Mother Lets Us Finish Our Projects

One of Mother's little quirks was that she was often overly accommodating. When visiting our house, back in the days when we had no guest room and she slept on the fold-out couch in the basement, she'd knock on the door at the top of the stairs before entering. She was often more apologetic than seemed appropriate, always bowing to others' wishes. Perhaps she'd learned this from her many years in our dysfunctional family. We never heard much about her own history as an only child, so it may have started even earlier!

This particular nature seemed to come in handy over the next couple of months: although she had come to the brink of death, she seemed to rock along at a fairly even pace for a while. The reason I'm "blaming" this on her accommodating nature is that all of her children (myself included) had important things on our calendars! After our visit, I went directly back to a children's grief camp and many other job-related responsibilities. My youngest sister had to have surgery (and recover from it). The oldest and her husband had waited many years to make some fairly substantial renovations to their home. Somehow, the major parts of the renovation, which would be terribly inconvenient to postpone, happened to fall during this time period.

So my dear, accommodating mother accommodated us all! Strange.

Certainly, many readers have heard stories of people waiting until the last child or sibling or parent or friend comes to visit before they take their last breath. Or, often, they may choose to be alone for their very private step through that portal. In this case, perhaps Mother was gracious enough to allow us kids to get a few more things off our own to-do lists. Interesting.

I told the hospice folks that they did not need to call me when they sensed Mother's death getting close. I felt as if I had been able to say my goodbyes. We even had the "dress rehearsal" of her dying with us present as a family. We were able to comfort one another, share those special moments, cry together. It was beautiful. I didn't feel the need to repeat the scenario. I'm good. Not necessary. Thank you very much.

Mother apparently had other ideas.

When all our calendars started clearing and the "optimal time" seemed to be approaching, I had more phone conversations with "number one daughter." My oldest sister graciously declared, "Okay, she can go now." Sounds crass, but we all realized how limited Mother's existence had been for the last few years. She enjoyed life, particularly after Father was gone (sorry, Father, but that's the truth, and I'm glad you're happy now on the Other Side). These last few years, however, her quality of life was definitely lacking.

I don't believe I could be so matter-of-fact about this were it not for my 150% belief in life after death. I don't know when I became so sure about a life after death; I can't recall a time when I didn't believe. There's no clear explanation of why or how I became so clearly convinced of life after death, no moment of conversion, per se. Call it intuitive, an "inner-knowingness," whatever you like. And it's my own belief—no one had to convince me. On some deep, deep level, I know; and I believe I've "always" known. I do believe I catch glimpses and feelings of a "world beyond," at least in my dreams!

Of course, most of my life I've attended church, where heaven is often talked about. But I didn't have any clear visual image of a heaven. Instead I just had a firm conviction that there was/is indeed something/someplace that our soul, spirit, essence moves to when it leaves the physical body. I sense the essence is something very real. And that essence cannot be obliterated. It simply can't. Somehow I know it and believe it. Deeply.

And I have sufficient moments in my own life in which I feel almost out of my body—enough that I know deeply and personally that the physical is indeed a container of sorts. I'm grateful for the container. Without it I wouldn't have the opportunity to experience this glorious life of the magnificent senses—sight, sound, touch, taste, smell. They're amazing! And I'm indeed grateful for each one! But for anything beyond those five senses, a physical body may not be necessary. Think about that for a moment. Even "thinking"—hmmm . . . is that possible without our physical body? Intriguing, isn't it?

I suggested that my sister take a Healing Touch Practitioner friend of hers to visit Mother and offer Healing Touch, if Mother were indeed ready to transition. She had taken the same friend with her months before to visit Mother, with the underlying purpose of preparing her for death. Though Mother rarely spoke, the instant this gal walked into the room, Mother seemed to know why she was there (i.e., to help her begin the dying process). She said, "I'm not ready." Okay, never mind!

This time, I asked that they call me when they were going so that I could be mentally, spiritually, and emotionally present with them during the time they were with her some 330 miles away. This time Mother did not reject her; however, nothing significant happened.

That morning, Mother came to me in a dream again. I thought perhaps it was a sign she would accept the gal and her offering of Healing Touch. Or not. As the week progressed, I once again had my "heartlight" turned on. She was calling me home. Okay, Mother, I'll see what I can work out.

In June, when she almost died the first time, others asked about her and how old she was. I'd reply, "If she makes it to her birthday, she'll be 87." I didn't really believe she'd make it to her birthday. Well, the day the Healing Touch gal visited her was a Sunday, two days after her birthday. By the end of

Monday, I had decided I had to go. All during the week, I kept mentally asking Mother to please wait till Friday. *I'll be home Friday. I'll be home Friday.*

I wanted to arrive during the day to see some of the hospice folks again. I'd arranged to be off that Friday and the following Monday and Tuesday. I told my husband, "If she's not dead by Tuesday, I'm coming home." It sounds very shallow, perhaps thoughtless, but I sincerely believed she had invited me to help her die. Sincerely. And last time, it didn't take that long to help get her started on that path!

Thursday night, my older sister called me. She had been to visit Mother earlier that evening. Mother was unresponsive when she visited, so she spoke with Mother's roommate. She told the roommate, "My sister Ruth will be here tomorrow." Her roommate said, "Good, because Ann has been asking for her again." The week before I visited Mother in June, she had been speaking in her sleep, asking for me. She was doing it again. And this was a woman who normally spoke very little. Perhaps she really had been visiting me during our nighttime wanderings.

Perhaps there really are layers and levels of consciousness in which we can connect with one another on some alternative plane of existence. At minimum, I believe she truly was visiting me in my dreams, just as I had invited her to do.

One funny thing: On Wednesday of that week, when the hospice aide had come to bathe her, Mother spoke a complete sentence! We used a dry erase board to communicate among visitors, so the aide had written on the board what Mother told her. She had said, "Go away, I didn't order your services!" My, my, aren't we persnickety! Not always so accommodating, I suppose.

Chapter 8: Take Two

When I arrived on Friday (a full eight weeks after her last near death experience), I greeted Mother, touching her hand and kissing her cheek. She said, "You're warm," and attempted to smile. She seemed to want to sit up, so I adjusted her hospital bed to help her. She asked for some water, saying "please" and "thank you." Always polite. I was a little surprised by how many words she'd already shared! The hospice chaplain was nearby when I arrived, so she joined us. After the chaplain sat down, she observed Mother scratching her head, and suggested that I offer to brush her hair. Great idea! Mother even responded, "I'd like that!" I opened the little drawer next to her bed and found two brushes. Oh dear. Which shall I choose? They were very different, so I made a random guess and picked one. As I gently stroked her hair, I asked, "Does that feel better?" She smiled, almost chuckled. "No." Oops. Wrong brush. The chaplain teased, "Nice try!" Okay, so I grabbed the other brush. "Is that better?" Mother smiled again. "Yes." We all smiled.

I can't describe what I was feeling. It was as if Mother had returned from some far-away place she'd been visiting for years, leaving her body behind and barely attended by a piece of her soul. This Mother felt familiar, a gift of presence I had not expected. A blessing.

I noticed the balloon attached to her bedside rail. It was a birthday balloon, brightly colored, wishing her "Happy Birthday" in bold letters. It was a helium balloon, floating proudly beside her. Yes, she made it to 87—quite an accomplishment! I asked her if she remembered Charlie, our orange tabby cat. I shared the story of how sweet Charlie got scared by a helium balloon, assuming I was really telling the story to the chaplain. I explained how Charlie inadvertently got the balloon string caught in his collar. Scared of the monstrous balloon, he ran as fast as he could up and down the hallway, trying to escape its menacing grasp and finally shaking it free. I had to observe this sight helplessly due to his unstoppable, frantic pace. When he finally broke free, he unfortunately was emotionally scarred forever; he now transfers his fear to anything and everything that vaguely resembles a balloon, including garbage bags, large handbags, etc.

And you'll never believe who was listening to me share sweet Charlie's adventures. Not just the chaplain. No, Mother apparently heard—and understood—every word. She was laughing. She got it! Unbelievable!

The chaplain had to leave after a little while. I mentioned that I should call my sisters and let them know how present Mother was. But at that point her eyes were beginning to look glassy again. I asked her, "Are you leaving again?" "Uh-huh," she replied. I said, "You like it when you leave, don't you?" "Uh-huh," she replied once again. And then she was gone. She took leave from this plane one more time.

I believe that was my first actual experience of watching Mother "come and go." I believe she could be very present with me, and then she could go away again. Where did she go? I don't really know, because I couldn't exactly go with her. However, I have some hunches. I believe she somehow managed to meet me during the night, when my consciousness would take flight as well. Perhaps she went off into the cosmos somewhere, perhaps into other realms of existence that I only seemed to glimpse in my dreams . . . perhaps to the place we call "heaven." She managed to stay connected to her body somehow, connected enough to return. She wasn't yet ready to leave—to "graduate"—completely. Not yet.

The "graduation" reference is one I started using after another dream I had with Mother years ago. In that dream, Mother had informed me she was getting ready to graduate, implying that she would just go ahead and do it, knowing I had a busy schedule and probably would not be able to attend. "No, Mother. I want to be there to see you graduate!" "Okay, let's look at your calendar." So, looking at my work calendar, she picked a time. I admit to having a bit of an obsession with numbers, so, I believe it was 11-11, at 11 a.m. I don't recall the exact year her graduation was originally planned for. But I did let her know I wanted to be in attendance! And we arranged for this in a dream, perhaps foretelling things to come. Perhaps.

Chapter 9: She's Back and Talking!

I visited on Saturday during the daytime, but she was not very responsive. Since her roommate had shared with me about her talking during the night (whether she was awake or asleep, we don't really know), I decided to come back later, after she and her roommate had been "tucked in" for the night, to see if anything interesting would come up. It was indeed interesting.

When I showed up, she said, "It's cold, you need to get a sweater." I gave her a kiss, and she giggled a little. She asked, "What day is it? I thought you were going to stay longer." Later, she said, "I'm going to have to go somewhere . . . are you going to do it for me?" (These are direct quotes—I was so fascinated by how much of Mother was present that I started taking notes!)

Mother has always been very expressive, particularly with her face. At one point she grimaced and said, "We don't understand one another." She later repeated it, "We don't understand one another." (Was she referring to me? Or perhaps to another "presence" of which she was aware?) Then she asked me if I wanted her to get up.

Her roommate walked by Mother's bed on the way back from the bathroom. She had on a blue bathrobe. As she passed, Mother said, "There's Miss Blue—you know her, don't you?" I don't think she had spoken a name (other than in her sleep or in her night-time speaking, based on her roommate's report) for more than a year. And to hear "Miss Blue," which was the name of one of her parakeets, was surprising. Was she referring to her roommate? Or did she possibly see a vision of her deceased parakeet? Who knows!

Later, she said, "I can't see. I can't hear . . . or know." I told Mother, "I'll do whatever you want me to do—I want you to be free of this body, free to dance with the angels." I then read from the Bible, selecting Psalm 23 (I started from memory, but then got emotional and began stumbling over the words). She was staring at me and declared, "You're going away." I asked if she wanted me to stay. I asked if she were cold. "Yes, aren't you?" I asked if she wanted me to tuck her in. "Yes." I reminded her that this was like how she often tucked us in as children. Then I leaned down to kiss her goodbye and said, as she had said so often to us, her children, "Goodnight, goodbye, and I love you."

When Mother went back to work after staying home with us kids for as many years as they could manage financially, she had to get up so early that my oldest sister was left with the responsibility of getting us up and ready in the mornings. Consequently, when we said our goodnights, it was also goodbye until the next evening. A bittersweet memory.

Before I left, her roommate turned out her light, which made the whole room (which was very tiny) very dark. Mother seemed startled. "What just happened?" she asked. She was able to close her eyes again and drift off to sleep, so I did the Healing Touch technique again. I also shared some words a friend had suggested (she believed it was from the Buddhist tradition, but wasn't quite sure). The words are as follows:

You come from Light, you are Light, you return to Light.
You come from Light, you are Light, you return to Light.
You come from Light, you are Light, you return to Light.
You come from God, you are God, you return to God.
You come from God, you are God, you return to God.

You come from God, you are God, you return to God.

You come from Love, you are Love, you return to Love.

You come from Love, you are Love, you return to Love.

You come from Love, you are Love, you return to Love.

Wherever these words are from, they're lovely, and I believe also very True, with a capital *T*.

Almost immediately, her breathing started to change and she began taking pauses again. I began to count: 18 seconds between breaths, 20, 40. . . . Then her eyes suddenly popped open, and she looked at the balloon and pushed the covers away. Her eyes closed again and she took 17 strong breaths, then went to 17–24 seconds in between—but this time it didn't get any worse, so I decided to go get some rest.

Chapter 10: Even More of Her Personality Is Showing

The next morning I returned. This time I thought I'd try some music to see if that would help her relax. I even brought headphones. I thought maybe she really didn't hear! After all, her saying, "I can't hear, I can't see" might have been literal. She had worn glasses and hearing aids before she forgot what they were for. Now she had neither. I played my music and asked her if she liked it. She said, "Yes," though I don't have a clue if she realized it was her daughter Ruth who was singing. Then later she said, "That was bad!" Okay, so now she's a music critic!

At one point she squirmed, trying to raise herself up on the bed and saying, "My back is red." I asked if it hurt. "Yes." So I applied lotion to her bony back. Another time, she asked me to scratch her back for her. She had been bedbound for weeks by then. They had removed her wheelchair from the room because she no longer had the strength to deal with transferring back and forth. She also was eating less and less. She would still take water, but her food choices were random, primarily yogurt and very soft, cool foods.

That day she was barely responsive after her request for attention to her back. She had some ice cream for lunch and some sips of milk. Nothing for supper. That evening she looked at me and asked, "My mother?"

I began drafting a eulogy, or at least words describing her life. It's hard to summarize a human being, isn't it? A life is so complex, it's impossible to cram it into lines and phrases. So we tell stories. Yes, I'll tell stories. Mother stories. And I began:

Elizabeth Ann

Ann grew up in Missouri. She served in the Coast Guard, where she began her career with the federal government. She married Tom in 1947. They had four children, two of whom were born in Columbia, while she and Tom were students at the University of Missouri. Ann got a bachelor's degree in home economics and a couple of little girls as well.

They moved a lot while the girls were young, adding two more children to the picture just one year apart. Life in their household wasn't boring . . .

Chapter 11: "This Is Her Day"—Or Is It?

On Monday, I walked in to find the hospice nurse sitting in a chair beside Mother's bed, smiling. She apparently had discovered an active version of Mother this morning, following the fairly unresponsive version that was here yesterday. Having been down this road with many folks before, our dear hospice nurse saw this as the burst of energy so often observed prior to death. That morning she asked if all the "arrangements" (i.e., funeral and burial arrangements) had been made. She also made the statement that it was a privilege to be present for days like this. "It almost makes my heart explode!" she declared, smiling. She then left the room to locate the hospice chaplain. She said, "Today, it's spiritual issues that need attention, not physical."

I suppose many hospices distribute literature describing the end-of-life changes that frequently occur. Though not a precise blueprint, it does prove helpful at times. The nurse was very quick to say, however, that she quit trying to predict timetables for families a long time ago, realizing that every person is different, every family situation is different.

Today, Mother was very talkative. She was asking questions, seemingly about death and/or heaven. She even asked, "What am I supposed to do in heaven?" She asked, "What do I do with my feet?" I explained (as if I knew!! Ha!), "You won't need them in heaven." She giggled, looking surprised. Some of the things she said did not make much sense (to me, at least, since I'm still rather attached to this earthly form!).

It feels odd for me to say that, considering this was a woman who had barely said anything at all for a year or more. However, the gal who had been showing up lately had been making sense, for the most part!

Strangely, in the middle of asking about food in heaven and saying things like, "You can't get it out . . . get it out of here . . . I tried and it's not working," she made a very mean-looking face and said, "You're in my way!" After the nurse left, she once said, "Scat!" with a very angry face. Later, she said, "I'm gonna get you!" then changed back to a friendly face, as if she were teasing. She even told me I smelled good!

She mentioned she was going to see her mother and daddy. She was smiling about that. She seemed to be interacting at times with unseen forces. She asked, "Can you see that?" I told her I wish I could. I tried to get her to describe what or whom she was seeing. "Do you recognize anyone? Are they wearing robes? Clothes? Are they human? Are they angels?" She didn't share. I remember telling her that we wanted her to be comfortable. She replied, "Comfortable? Not where I'm going." What?

She did say—more than once—"Let's go!" She was ready and she was excited. I suggested that we hold hands and reached for hers. I explained that when she was ready, I'd give her hand to Jesus and let him take her the rest of the way. (Jesus was a very central being in Mother's life; she in fact had a vision of Jesus many years earlier, when she was totally "with it.")

Chapter 12: Things Get Even MORE Interesting!

My brother-in-law stopped by for his usual Monday visit. When he walked into the room, Mother said, "I recognize your voice." Then she told him, "I'm having trouble getting away!" She then added, "You can't help me do this." I told her I wanted to help. I snuggled up with her, but she eventually pushed me away, laughing, "You're hot!" Not long after, she made a mean face again, saying, "Get!" Soon, she was grinning again. Teasing? I'm not sure.

The reason I'm not sure if she was teasing or not is that it felt different at times. In my notes, I wrote, "Did she let someone else in there?" It may sound bizarre, but I was wondering if—in her "out-of-body" experiences on those other planes—another spirit or soul could sneak in and share her space, so to speak. One of my quirks is that I have a very broad view of the universe. I believe lots of things are possible. This experience of having my mother "back" after being gone for so many years was amazing enough. The possibility that another presence might want to keep her body alive was suddenly becoming "real."

Perhaps one of the reasons Mother sought me out to help her with dying is because I do feel and intuit a lot. I'm sensitive to lots of things— especially energies. I don't "see" like some folks do (as in auras, etc.), and I'm not clairvoyant or clairaudient. However, I am sometimes aware of other layers and levels. Maybe that's one of the reasons I was invited to this party!

When we were alone that day, Mother mentioned that the "helpers are here." The helpers? She used the word "helpers" several times. Again, my curiosity was working overtime, desperate for some concrete images to share! At least I had a new word! I'd never heard anyone refer to "helpers" before. My sense was that the helpers were there to help her cross over. So, again, I suggested that we join hands with the helpers. I reached for her hand with my left hand and reached out my right hand to the invisible forces in the room. Shockingly, I felt a real hand in my right hand! At that moment, my older sister had walked into the room and placed her hand in mine. What timing! Mother was delighted that she had joined us. She said, "You go with me!" I explained that we could only go with her so far. At some point we'd need to give her hand to Jesus or to one of the helpers, who would help her the rest of the way. She said, "Okay."

But we didn't go anywhere.

Later on, she asked if I'd scratch her back, but said, "You can't do it long." I reassured her, "Yes, I can." Then in a bit she asked, "Does your head hurt like mine?" I asked her, "Does your head hurt?" "Yes, I guess not so bad." Then I asked her, "Do you hurt in other places?" "Yes." I asked her where it hurts. "I don't know." I asked again, "But you do hurt?" "Yes." Then Mother said, "I guess I can sleep." I asked her if she wanted to sleep to make the hurt go away. "Yes," she replied. I told her they could give her some medicine to help the hurt go away. Is that all right? She said, "Yes."

So, that afternoon, for the first time, I told the nurse she was talking about hurting. The nurse said, "Good call," because Mother was not the type to complain—about anything.

What concerns me—as a human being and as a hospice person—is that there seems to be a whole generation of folks who are not complainers. They are the ones who "bear up" under pain. The goal of hospice is comfort at the end of life. Had I not been with her for so many hours, we might not

even have realized she had any pain at all. Instead she
simply would have "gone away" (to her alternative reality),
perhaps to avoid any physical pain remaining in her body.

She had had a big day, so before it was really night, she said a couple of times, "Let's just all go to bed!" So I sang to her, like at bedtime, singing one of the songs she sang to me as a child.

Strangely, although my mother was not in a sorority in
college, the song she chose was the Sigma Chi sweetheart
song. The part she sang to us goes something like this:

The girl of my dreams is the sweetest girl of all the girls I know.
Each sweet co-ed like the rainbow trail fades in the afterglow.
The blue of her eyes and the gold of her hair are a blend of the Western sky,
And the moonlight beams on the girl of my dreams, she's the sweetheart of Sigma Chi.
("The Sweetheart of Sigma Chi," words by Byron D. Stokes, Albion, 1913)

Yes, Sigma Chi. I haven't a clue as to the significance of that!
The best guess I can make is that we all started off as blue-

eyed blondes (we kept our blue eyes but not our blonde hair).
When I gave birth to my blue-eyed blonde daughter, I sang
the same song to her, making it more politically correct by
substituting something like, "She's my sweetheart, I can't
deny." I think that's what I substituted; but, just like with my
own mother, it was the sound and the experience of mother
and daughter snuggling, not the words, that truly created the
magic of that so-called lullaby!

And here we are, mother and daughter, sharing a precious
moment in time, blending beginnings and endings, giving and
receiving, frozen in space and time, two females eternally
bonded by some profoundly cosmic connection.

And then, I turned more traditional and sang "In the
Garden." And yes, my head was hurting too.

Chapter 13: Mother Gets a Little Ornery

We were having these magical, memorable moments (Mother had her eyes shut, as if she were "traveling" again), when one of the nursing home gals came to check to see if Mother needed changing. She was dry; so, as required, the gal took a permanent marker and began to write on her diaper. Mother woke up, startled, saying in a voice just as clear and audible as the one she raised to us children quite often, "What are you doing?" The sweet gal (who said Mother reminded her of her own grandmother—usually, that is) responded, teasingly, "Why, Miss Ann, I'm writing on your belly." Mother actually slapped her and said, "You're sick!" Whoa! Fortunately, she didn't have much strength in her swing. I quickly apologized for her. And, from then on, I warned the gals who followed!

I then learned, from her roommate, that Mother had not always been the best behaved patient. She had bitten and hit some of the staff at times. It was not predictable. One change which seemed to help early on—before she was totally bedbound—was to alter her morning wake-up time. Mother had always been a night owl. She loved staying up reading or watching the late show on television. So, when they didn't insist on waking her up at the crack of dawn, she did indeed seem much happier. I'd imagine that's one of the hazards of nursing home care. You end up—for the most part—having to conform to a generic kind of schedule, which is often not your own.

I shared that I'm sensitive to energy types of things. A "signal" I began getting after my father died in 1983 was something I call a "chill." Some people call it goosebumps. When it comes on out of the blue, I usually identify it as "confirmation." It will usually follow a thought or a declaration of some kind (or a "guess" about something). It also sometimes seems to indicate a "presence" of sorts. My father was the first person close to me who died. I say "close" to indicate that he played a prominent role in my life. Sadly, I never truly felt close to him emotionally. That was difficult (if not impossible) for him. He just wasn't wired that way. So perhaps, when his "energy" changed to spirit, he was able to touch me differently. Just a theory. That's when I began to be aware of the seemingly random "chills."

Can I explain the energy surge? Nope. But I feel it. And others have shared that they feel it as well. It seems like it was years before others shared the "goosebump/chill" thing with me. But once that door opened, I discovered I was most definitely not alone in recognizing the feeling or in using it as a barometer of confirmation. When Mother seemed to be resting (eyes closed), I would often get a very distinct chill. Was this some kind of sign? I don't know. Perhaps on some level I knew one of her "helpers"? Maybe. Maybe not. Maybe Mother was waving goodbye as she went to visit the other plane or dimension—or heaven.

This was still the same day the helpers came. At one point I asked her if the helpers were still there. "No." Later, when she seemed restless, squirming, I asked if some medicine might help her feel better. She said, "It doesn't seem to make any difference." Quite a sentence for someone who said almost nothing for a year or so, isn't it? However, up to this point, all she'd been getting was acetaminophen. Perhaps something different would allow her to sleep better.

Later on, after she seemed to sleep awhile, I asked if she'd like me to brush her hair. "That would feel good." Later, I asked if she'd like some ice cream, to which she replied, enthusiastically, "Yes!"

Because of all the amazing happenings of this day, when Mother asked my sister and me to go with her (we assumed to heaven), I asked if we should call our other sister or not. Hesitant to jump to any conclusions (we didn't want to needlessly "cry wolf" again), we simply called and asked her to come by on her way home from work. She did.

Later that afternoon, my oldest sister brought some sandwiches and sent me downstairs to get a soft drink. When I returned, my younger sister had arrived and they both were seated on the opposite side of the tiny room from where Mother lay, again non-responsive. We shared a sandwich and some light conversation. The oldest had experienced Mother in her more "present" form earlier in the day, while my younger sister still hadn't. I asked if she wanted to talk with Mother. "No, leave her alone. It's okay. She's always like this with me." Of course, I couldn't accept that. So after our meal was complete, I walked over to Mother's bedside, touched her hand, and called, "Mother." Her eyes opened and she was back.

"Come on over," I invited the others to join me. We talked and laughed, including Mother in the conversation. She participated nonverbally and some verbally as well. Both sisters shared what they were up to. When the younger one decided she had to go get some rest before getting up very early the next morning, she reached down to say goodbye and Mother began to cry. Of course, since tears are contagious, my sister also began to weep. She asked, "Do you want me to stay?" Mother responded as if she were a friend who had been in a foreign country for a long time, with something like, "Yes! Tell me about yourself!" My sister then proceeded to share what her life had been like for the last couple of years. Amazing. Incredible. A gift. At one point we invited our brother into the conversation via the telephone. We didn't want to leave him out just because of a couple hundred miles of physical distance. This was far too precious an experience to miss out on.

And we gals all held hands and prayed, something like:

Dear God, this precious child of yours is ready for her journey. Thank you for blessing us with her. Thank you for allowing us to be a part of her family. We ask that you welcome her once again into your heavenly family . . . welcome her home into your loving arms. She has been a gift to us. And we are ready to let her go and be with you. Thank you, oh loving and gracious God. Thank you.

My sister shared stories, not just current ones but stories from the last few years. It truly felt as if Mother were catching up on all the time she'd been mentally and/or spiritually "away." When my sister eventually decided she would have to leave, they both shed a few more tears. What a remarkable evening. What an amazing day!

Mother later did ask, "Where am I?" I said, "You're at home." Of course, with all the journeying in and out of this physical world, I believe I'd be a bit disoriented, too! She also asked me later who I was. "Ruth." "Who?" "Ruth, your middle girl." "Oh."

Well, it was Monday, and what a Monday it was! Mother was still blessing us with her presence; however, all indications pointed to her wish to "exit." But how soon? Tuesday was the original "deadline" I'd set for myself. (Remember, I'd told my husband, "If she's not dead by Tuesday, I'll be home.") But I couldn't leave—not just yet. It seemed like her exit might be just around the corner. I could stay a little longer.

Chapter 14: More Questions, Comparisons, Reflections

Fortunately, the only "vacation" I'd taken was my last trip to be with Mother in June, so I still had some paid time off coming. I could still manage a day or two or three, if I had to. I decided to stay.

The next day, when Mother seemed to be sleeping, I leaned down to whisper in her ear, "You come from God," beginning the prayer/chant. She opened her eyes and said, "I can't hear you." I tried again. She must have heard the word, "God," so she asked, "Are you talking to me or God?" I answered, "You, I guess."

What's a bit humorous (and I didn't think about this connection till later) was that my father was very persnickety (in fact, he was diagnosably obsessive-compulsive, I do believe). Mealtimes had a few basic rituals attached to them, one being his prayer at the beginning of the meal. Most folks might read this and say, "Oh, that's nice." Well, the truth is that his ritual was to speak the prayer so fast that the words weren't even recognizable. If we asked him what he'd said, he'd reply, "I wasn't talking to you!"

I wonder if Mother, in her moments of clarity, had any recollection at all of this!

Later on, I asked her if she hurt anywhere, to which she answered, "Yes." However, she managed a fairly peaceful smile most of the time. When I surprised her with a kiss, saying, "Gotcha," she giggled, saying, "No, you don't!"

Around lunchtime, I asked if she were hungry. Did she want anything to eat? She'd been taking only occasional spoonfuls of anything. In fact, since I was trying to be as thrifty as possible on this journey, I'd eat just about anything they brought me from the kitchen. That itself was an experience!

My younger sister joined us later that day. Mother actually said, "No, thank you," to ice cream, but did ask for water. It wasn't till around 8 p.m. that evening, when I asked her if she wanted more water, that she said, emphatically, "I want supper!" We had to improvise, but, for her, some yogurt and/or juice would usually suffice. After her overly indulgent meal of a container of yogurt, she drifted off to sleep. I did a little

Healing Touch, a little praying, and called it a night. Of course, she started what I would call "intermittent breathing," but for Mother, that was apparently not a sign of any significant change. It was perhaps only an indication of sound sleep (or maybe a little bit of that astral traveling!).

The next morning, I went in to find that Mother had managed to feed herself bites of a donut and tiny pieces of a strip of bacon. *Oh my, Mother, you're full of surprises.* She seemed understandably worn out. Digestion is no laughing matter! I expended a little energy myself trying to arrange some classical music so she could hear it.

She and Father were huge fans of "serious" music, as he called it. He refused to call it generically "classical" because the Classical Period was only one period in musical history. I tried a radio, then a computer with recorded music. During the whole effort, I felt a few tears appear. Memories from childhood were flooding my consciousness. Our house was filled with music when I was growing up. Despite the dysfunction, a love of music remained in each one of us. For moments, I caressed her, holding her much like she held each one of us, in her arms. Tears are warm, aren't they?

Meanwhile, the hospice aide had not yet arrived. Mother asked me, "Is it time to get up?" Later, she exclaimed, "I'm never going to get out of here!" to which she added, "I can't get my shoes off. I'll just have to wear them." I suppose she was referring to the trip she was about to make. (I also recalled her earlier question about what we do with feet in heaven!)

She was more restless than usual, picking and pulling at things. The hospice nurse had finally convinced the doctor to prescribe an anti-anxiety medicine as well as liquid morphine, to be used as needed. Of course, the trick was to discern when and if they were needed. I shared that she appeared to be somewhat agitated, waving her arms a lot, picking at her nose and the hairs on her chin—pretty much anything her left hand could grab (the right one was still very contracted). So they gave her the anti-anxiety medicine plus acetaminophen.

She asked another question, as if I were the expert. "Will there be girls?" Again, I assumed her questions were about her journey into the afterlife. "Girls? Women? Yes. Absolutely!"

She was able to rest, which was wonderful. I did more Healing Touch.

I flashed onto my experience of labor and delivery with my own daughter. I'd never made the connection before now.

Yes, there truly is a comparison. Before joining Mother in this adventure, I had observed that hospice nurses were like midwives, assisting in "birthing" people into the next world. Of course, I also discovered I wasn't the first to consider that analogy. (There are books written about it!) However, I was following it even further.

My labor of birthing my own precious baby lasted "forever." (I realize 36 hours is not forever, but it sure was long enough!) My hope was that, when Mother finally was able to relax with the help of medication, perhaps she could relax enough to let go. When I had accepted the help of an epidural, I began dilating and was able to deliver a beautiful baby girl. One of my first days here with Mother, I dreamed of benzodiazepines (drugs often prescribed for anxiety), which was totally strange. Perhaps this was why. Perhaps she needed to have some anti-anxiety medication in order to relax, in order to let go.

Later, the hospice aide came to bathe her, wash her hair, and tuck her in. I went to do laundry, since I hadn't packed for this long a stay. When I returned, she looked so peaceful and calm. Even a sponge bath can be exhausting. It may have been pure exhaustion instead of calmness!

During these many hours with Mother, I often reflected on cosmic kinds of issues. Today I was reflecting on time and space. They're manufactured to serve us—how? Time seems to be merely a measuring stick. Aren't there enough of those already? And space—a separation, really. I think I may need some sleep . . . I'm getting a bit philosophical! Or is it theological? By this time, I had moved from my older sister's house (which was torn up for renovation) into my younger sister's (she was recovering from surgery). At night, when I'd go "home," the first thing I'd do was readjust the thermostat (all of us had been raised to be fairly environmentally conscious, so we don't over-cool in the summer, even in this exceptionally hot August). Then I'd often (not always) pour myself a small glass of red wine and sit on the porch and howl at the moon. Actually, I did more reflecting than howling. And I did do a lot of cloud gazing and star gazing. And praying. Praying for a peaceful transition for Mother. I also used that time for phone calls, if it wasn't too late. Calling my California cousin was usually an option, since they're in an earlier time zone.

I've been very attached to skies since childhood (I share a little about that in my book The Prescription for Joy*). Gazing at the stars and the clouds has always been a way for* *me to breathe in the fullness and joy of being one of God's beloved children. The whole "parental" image of God resonated with me on a very profound level as I walked this walk with Mother.*

By now it was Wednesday (I still hadn't been with her a full week). Meanwhile, Mother's roommate and I were becoming friends. Her roommate was a sweet, gentle soul. She herself had hoped to die years earlier! She shared her disappointment about having "graduated" from hospice. She was not at all happy that she had had cancer and it was in remission. Being a natural listener and a psychotherapist by trade, I ended up encouraging so many of these little conversations (particularly during periods when Mother was non-responsive) that she soon began stopping to chat on her way to and from the bathroom. I had asked about the times when Mother talked in her sleep before my arrival. This time her roommate shared more of what she had said the last time (before this visit). Mother had said, "This isn't the way it's supposed to end!" Of course, there could be many interpretations of those words, but the one I would consider is that she did not want to die alone in a nursing home.

By later that night, she began doing the breathing thing again.

Chapter 15: Her Body Just Won't Quit!

The next day, we were visited by all the hospice folks—the nurse, the social worker, and two chaplains. They added a male chaplain to the team because Mother responded more to the male than to the female. Our theory was that, in her older years, Mother had become a bit of a flirt! (Our father had died 26 years earlier and she never remarried.) So, Mother had a full day. She even mentioned the farm, something I'd never really heard much about. I asked if she saw her mother and daddy. "No . . . people . . . people." Later, she became restless. Her heart rate jumped to 125 bpm. Whoa! I could see her pulse thumping in her throat. Her belly rumbled and gyrated as if it were going to explode.

The hospice nurse offered the hospice room. A hospice room? What does that mean? One of the challenges of being a hospice patient in a nursing home is that you are preparing to die in a place where they had been committed to keeping you alive. Opposing forces, so to speak. It's hard to get everyone "on board." Plus, on this particular floor, there was a lot of noise. There were buzzers going off constantly. I suppose because the same patients/residents repeatedly rang the buzzers for assistance, their calls were often ignored. Perhaps the staff became numb to their incessant ringing. I, on the other hand, never was able to ignore it. If Mother needed something, I never rang the buzzer. I always walked up the hall and asked for it myself. It was simpler that way.

A hospice room, if available, would be private. That would be an advantage. If she were in a private home or a private room, at least we would have some control over the environment. At this point, however, the hospice room was not available. There was already a family with a hospice patient utilizing the room. Perhaps it would eventually be an option. However, I continued to think she would be leaving us soon. After all, we continued to see daily changes. And, as I've heard our own hospice nurses say, "When the changes are weekly, they have weeks left. When the changes are daily, they have days left. When the changes are hourly . . ."

The nursing home chaplain came by. Mother brightened up. He was a handsome older man, with a striking white beard and a gentle demeanor. He asked, "Shall I share a prayer?" She said, "Go ahead." He spoke his own prayer, then the Lord's Prayer, then made the sign of the cross on her forehead.

Later that day she told me, "I'm sorry you came home." Then, "Earlier we had ____, didn't we?" "Had what?" "You know." I came home because she called me home, as in *E.T.* It was very right for me to be there with her. That's what I told her. She then said, "Hold me." I did.

She had been cold, but by early afternoon, she was hot and "clammy." As I was touching her skin, Mother moved her hand and scratched me with one of her fingernails. "Did I hurt you?" she asked. "Yes!" Then she said, "I'm gonna kick you every time!" and she smiled—teasing again, I suppose.

That evening, she was hurting, and she could even identify where this time—in her hips. They gave her a first dose of morphine and later gave her more anti-anxiety medicine for agitation. We were having random bits of conversation—clearly understandable words, but not always clearly understandable thoughts.

While on morphine, she asked if I had talked to so-and-so. I asked if she wanted me to talk to someone, and if so, who. "I don't know who." Later, when I was touching her, she asked if I needed a sweater. So I asked her if she needed another blanket.

No, she was fine. She was still my mother. She was worried about me being cold.

Just like when I delivered my sweet baby girl, I stayed through three separate shifts of nurses, only to return to the original on-duty nurse. That nurse didn't expect us to be there when she returned. And, just like finding out the hospice room wasn't available to us when we felt we were ready, the birthing room hadn't been available to us either. Similarities.

The hospice nurse came in again before she left the building. Mother was pulling her knees up and down restlessly. She went to get more medicine. By the time she returned, Mother was non-responsive and her pulse was extremely high again.

Chapter 16: My Learning Continues

I was learning so much during this journey with Mother. I was also reflecting a lot on our life together and on what she taught me. There were funny little things—memories of how she showed me the cosmetic trick I use daily, i.e., smudging a bit of lipstick on my cheeks instead of actual blush (an automatic match of colors!). Another tip from Mother (as recent as 10-15 years ago!) was for making beds. She had a spiffy little way of putting pillow cases onto pillows. Love it! She was a shining example of courtesy, being polite even in her last days, when speaking words required precious energy. She always tried to make room for "please and thank you."

Another amazing thing: the more I gazed at her physical self, the more I realized how much we looked alike. I don't believe I'd realized how much we had in common physically. Probably a good year before, I had become more aware of my own sleeping patterns. I always sleep on my back, but I had begun sleeping with my left arm over my head, with my curled-up right hand against my cheek. As I touched the outside of my cupped hand, I would imagine Mother's touch and silently—to myself—speak to Mother, telling her I was imagining her touch. Little did I know that I would begin to really connect to Mother during the night. Much to my amazement, I discovered that Mother's favorite sleeping position was with her left arm raised above her head on her pillow. Her right hand was contracted.

She also gave me healthy hair and skin. And her hair seemed to have done what mine did. My sisters still had dark hair, peppered with gray. Mine became progressively lighter—all over! I would put temporary hair color on it every few months, but before I'd get around to it, it would look as if it had been highlighted—but still on the lighter side. Her hair was dark for many years, but gradually lightened (assisted by hair color, too, of course) through the years. Even our body shape was similar. Strange. It was almost as if I'd been unaware of the connection till all this happened. She was always there. She was always Mother. But the others needed her in ways that I didn't seem to. I was the one who left home at age 17. The other girls were there and had more *contact than I, understandably. That was all right. They seemed to have more of an emotional connection with her.*

Perhaps ours was a re-plugging-in of a spiritual connection (one that I never realized we had!).

Mother was now receiving morphine more often. I was there with her so often that I was observing subtle changes. For the staff, who only occasionally popped in, they were not discernable differences. For me they were. On one occasion, when Mother hadn't had any medication all night, I believed she needed something. I walked with the nurse's aide down the hall to the nurses' station (remember, I never felt comfortable ringing the buzzer, since they were often ignored). Apparently, the nurse didn't realize I was there. When the aide asked for more medication, she said, "I'll bet it's that daughter, isn't it?" in a very sarcastic tone. Later, when she realized I was standing there within earshot, she quickly changed her tone. She decided to come with me to check on Mother. Even though Mother looked as if she were resting, she still decided to ask her, "Are you hungry?" "No." "Are you thirsty?" "No." "Are you in pain?" "Yes." She was answering with her eyes closed, yet the nurse finally believed her. This particular nurse continued to resist giving her medication. Since the medicine was only ordered "as needed," it was left up to the nurses to decide when she needed it. That was a real roll of the dice!

That experience reminded me of the strict need for confidentiality and a respectful attitude toward patients and their families. This time I had been on the receiving end of negative comments. Fortunately, I didn't take it personally (although she may have meant it personally!). I shared it with the hospice nurse, who was quick to say she was usually one of the easiest and kindest nurses to work with. Go figure. She was probably tired that night. I was, too. We all still need to remain respectful—or at least tactful!

Another eye-opener for me was the variety of nursing styles and attitudes. Some were very open to giving morphine, trusting my input about changes in Mother's demeanor, etc. Others were very resistant. In my work in hospice care, I frequently hear stories from clients about doctors who simply refuse to offer hospice as an option, even when they freely admit there's nothing more they can do in a curative sense for the patient.

Perhaps it feels as if they are giving up.

It's truly a change in emphasis—from providing so-called curative care to providing as much comfort care as possible.

It isn't stopping their care. Instead, it's shifting to maximizing quality of life at the end of life, providing symptom and pain management. I believe that's a wonderful goal of care.

My experience with the end-of-life care Mother received was overall extraordinarily positive. Most of the challenges were in the interface between hospice and the medical doctor and nursing home care.

We don't talk about death nearly enough in our culture. And we need to be more proactive in our planning for the end of our own lives! Morbid? Personally, I don't think so. But, for whatever reason, I've always been one to embrace the fragility and finite nature of this physical life form we inhabit!

I totally understand how difficult it is to have those conversations about our own mortality. We are mortal creatures. Our physical selves do have their own "expiration date." Most of us can't predict when that is. But it will happen. Our physical bodies will eventually stop functioning. I do believe that we need to "gift" ourselves with those intimate conversations about our own mortality before an emergency or unexpected terminal diagnosis! I believe most of us would choose to have a more peaceful ending to our lives instead of being in a hospital environment, plugged into lots of machines.

The next day, an aide claimed that Mother ate some breakfast. However, when I got to the room, there was maybe one bite of donut gone—one tiny bite at best! She opened her eyes once, when I walked into the room, then closed them again. There was no sign of recognition. I had flashes of the movie *Testament*, in which a mother had to prepare her daughter's body for burial following a nuclear holocaust. I was watching this special person who gave me life, who birthed me into existence, leave this world.

We were once connected by an umbilical cord. Now we're connected in spirit. Soon we would "only" be connected in spirit.

Ironically, our father died right after he paid Mother's last car payment. Well, Mother's "housing" was paid for through that day. Shall I share the economic angle? Why not! I'd been asking for prayers for a peaceful transition, continually expecting each day to be her last. Why not try something new? She'd always been thrifty. She always had to make do with not so much. We'd had many periods of relative poverty. She probably didn't want to be an economic burden to anyone—not even the federal government (after all, she was a retired federal employee!). I gave it a try. I let her know that the money to pay for the nursing home was about to run out! No change. I felt a little silly.

That night, on the radio, I heard "Spirit in the Sky," a song about "where I'm gonna go when I die."

Chapter 17: Dreams Again Bring Instruction

The next morning (day nine), while drifting between dreamland and wakefulness, I saw an image of Mother's face, smiling. Cool. Peaceful-looking. However, when I got there, even though they gave her both medications not long after I arrived, she was doing her "pull-ups" (where she would try to pull her body over to the handrail). At midday, as she was finally calming down some, she closed her eyes and her heart rate soon jumped to a very violent feeling 125 bpm! Eventually a nurse checked her pulse officially and said it was indeed 125 bpm. She decided to give her some medicine. She was ready to rest.

During these days of watching and waiting with Mother, since I was not able to do much but sit with her, I took a couple of extended breaks at a local restaurant with free internet access. The first day I tried to take a break, I got a bit lost. I may have spent a lot of years in St. Louis, but I hadn't lived there for over 30 years! There had been a lot of changes in that time. I thought I was in the right place, but couldn't spot the restaurant. I called my local friend to ask for directions. She said, "You should be across the street from it!" We started talking. I shared my concern about Mother being in a room where her roommate had the radio on a lot. So, there were a lot of hours when it wasn't quiet. Plus, her roommate never left the room, so the theory that some people like to die alone would never get a chance to be tested. I would leave periodically, but her roommate was always there. My friend started asking questions about Mother's roommate. She began sharing stories of women she had befriended over the years. She came by later to visit and met Mother's roommate.

Lovely relationships can evolve with all kinds of folks! Nursing homes are filled with many who are still very conversational in addition to those who aren't. And there are many opportunities for surprising friendships to evolve. Just a thought to consider!

Soon after my friend left, I watched Mother's aggressively beating heart rate go from 125 bpm to a full stop. Her breathing also appeared to have stopped. Plus, she had pulled the balloon down and it was resting on her chest. Beautiful. Symbolic, perhaps? One more experience to add to the mix—energetically, there was a "whoosh" that almost knocked me over! I literally had to fall back into the chair. She's gone. She must be. I called my older sister, greeting her with scripture: "This is the day the Lord has made. Let us rejoice and be glad in it." However, by the time my sister asked, "Is she dead?" she had started breathing again. False alarm. Sorry. I think all the combined "signs" and all the dramatic changes led me to believe—all too quickly—that she was gone. Sorry.

The nurse came in not long after and checked her pulse. It was back to normal. My, what a roller coaster ride!

By late afternoon, however, her pulse was back up. Her belly was gyrating once again and the pulse point in her throat was practically jumping through her skin! Added to that, she started the breathing thing again. This time, she started with 35 second "breaks," building up to a full minute. *Mother! How are you doing this? You're the Energizer Bunny for sure. I'm tired, though. I need a nap!* "Wake me up to wave goodbye," I instructed her.

After a brief time of rest, I awoke to a steady pattern of 55–58 seconds between breaths. It was indeed like counting time between labor contractions. I found myself using the stopwatch on my phone. My younger sister chose to stay with me that night. Mother was having such a time, she thought it made sense to stay. So did I. In the middle of the night, an aide came in to change her. She was dry, and yet she changed her anyway. It seemed painful—Mother was groaning in discomfort; so we asked for more morphine. Fortunately, they agreed.

Just like during labor, I found myself nodding off between "contractions"!!

That morning (it was Sunday, day ten, by now), I waited till it was a reasonable time and called one of my own hospice nurses. I didn't want to bother Mother's hospice team—after all, it was the weekend! So instead, I bothered one of my hometown friends. Her take on giving Mother morphine was that you have to assume they're having pain when they're no longer able to tell you. At this point, Mother's heart rate had been over 120 bpm for almost 24 hours! I explained that our problem was convincing the nurses to give the morphine. Not being scheduled, it didn't show up on their screens. So even when we asked, the most often she was getting it was every five hours.

My sister and I decided to leave for a while, thinking, perhaps, that she was waiting for us to leave (since we'd stayed all night). When we returned, the aide (who had told us Mother reminded her of her own grandmother) had fed her. She was proudly proclaiming that Mother had had a couple of containers of cranberry juice, yogurt, and a little of the vanilla shake. She was proud of how much she'd been able to feed her! She did at least apologize for the little pieces of peach in the yogurt—she realized that might be challenging to Mother but fed it to her anyway. Mother, on the other hand, looked miserable. She had the most vacant stare I'd seen in days. Plus, she had her left hand stuck at her throat, one finger conveniently pointing to a major artery, as if she were taking her own pulse! She stayed posed in that uncomfortable-looking position, immovable, for approximately seven hours. Her body did not need the extra challenge of having to digest food at this point, I'm afraid. But the unknowing, well-intentioned staff person fed her "grandma." That's what you do, right? Wrong.

This is another example of the conflict between the nursing home staff, who were with her in her living, and the hospice staff, who were with her in her dying.

Chapter 18: Will She Ever Let Go?

I love the way that the right song just seems to show up on the radio. Call it coincidence. That's fine. But it may have been more than coincidence (or "cosmic coincidence") to awaken from a nap, hearing (in my head), "Sweet dreams are made of this," considering dreams had been a theme throughout my journey with Mother. On the way to my sister and brother-in-law's house, I heard a song (on the radio this time) which was new to me, which said, "It's too hard to leave you . . . I love you so." The next night, in the middle of the night, I awoke to the song "Tears on my pillow . . ."

When I next saw Mother, it was as if she had had another mini-stroke. Her left eye was fixed and the other was tracking. Bizarre to observe.

That night, I "felt" Mother throughout the night. In my dream, I was trying to find a home for a lamb. I was holding her in my arms. She had nails and I knew she might bite. But I was looking for a home for her. My mother, my lamb. Let's find you a home!

On my way to visit the nursing home earlier that evening, I heard songs on the radio: "Lost in a Dream," and a song with "Glory days . . . bring it home" in it. It ended with "Let's go!" Jeez, Mother, can you affect the airways?

The next evening, I believe I was awakened by Mother's "call." I felt she was inviting me to join her at the nursing home earlier this time. Perhaps she realized it was too noisy in the daytime. She showed us that this "leaving" business she was trying to do was more complicated than any of us had imagined, particularly because she had no specific disease affecting the functioning of her systems. Her heart, the only thing that had been even the least bit problematic, was almost taunting us, saying, "I can survive anything!"

I arrived and lay with her cuddled in my arms. She started the breathing thing again and was relaxing, seemingly beginning to drift gently away, when her face wrinkled into a terrified grimace and she said, "Hell!" Oh dear. I thought she was ready to go. Maybe not. Maybe there was still some fear blocking her exit. It was time to call in some "higher authorities." Following that Monday, when she had expressed some concern about "not needing to be comfortable where I'm going," I'd spoken off and on to her about forgiveness. I attempted to absolve her of anything and everything I was aware of. I guess we needed someone who counted a bit more than I did in the forgiveness department! Perhaps we'd try Communion. I had asked about it earlier, just because. This time we probably truly needed it.

Synchronistically, when the nursing home chaplain arrived with the Communion elements, her local pastor walked in the door as well. Her pastor had just come back from vacation and had decided to drop by the nursing home. Perfect timing! They knew one another and shared a very beautiful ritual of Communion with Mother. She was not visibly involved. In fact, the tiny piece of wafer was discovered later on, stuck in her teeth. However, there was no more mention of hell. Excellent.

The next morning Mother decided she needed me up even earlier!

Chapter 19: Mother Seems to Be Getting "Tricky"

This morning's dream was pretty random. I couldn't find any underlying purpose or profound meaning behind it, but I still faithfully wrote it down.

In the dream, the hospice social worker and I were together in a different room. We were chatting, trying to decide what we wanted to drink—coffee or tea. My sense was that she was more of a tea drinker. But that was the whole point of the dream—coffee or tea. Pleasant, but seemingly irrelevant or trivial.

I awoke, with the dream still hanging in my consciousness, to the sound of a *boing* and a *clunk*. The sound came from another room. It was around 3:30 or 3:45 a.m., so it was still dark. Using the light from my cell phone as my guide, I gingerly walked through one room to the next, looking for something that could have caused the sound. It sounded as if something had fallen to the floor. In the kitchen, I spotted the culprit. It was a spring-loaded rod (like the kind used for a shower curtain) with a small curtain hanging from it. It had popped free from the back door and fallen to the floor. There was no logical reason for it to fall, no precipitating event. It simply fell. I took a picture of the rod on the floor. Strange.

The timing was interesting. Since I had been in and out of the nursing home at odd hours, I had noticed on the front doors (which opened automatically, of course) a sign indicating the doors would be locked from 11 p.m. to 3:45 a.m. Was Mother aware of this? Had her spirit, in its travels through the ethers, somehow noticed the earliest time I could freely walk through those doors? *Okay, Mother, this is pretty early. You better have a good reason for getting me up!* I said to myself. I decided to call the nursing home. No way was I getting dressed at 3:30 in the morning if there was no change. No answer. Hmmm.

Okay, maybe getting me there at 7:30 a.m. yesterday morning just wasn't early enough. Maybe she believes she needs to get me there in the early morning hours so it would truly be quiet. So I walked through the doors at about 4:15 a.m., and was snuggled together with her by 4:30 a.m. In the next couple of hours, I did some Healing Touch, held her, and said prayers. I called upon the help of Jesus, Archangel Michael, even the Bodhisattva Quan Yin (from the Buddhist tradition—compassion and healing are her specialties!).

Fortunately, the previous night I had literally hit my "wall" at about 9 p.m. (definitely earlier than usual), so I had actually gone home and headed straight to bed. Otherwise, I might not have even noticed the thump when the curtain rod fell to the floor!

When her roommate made a trek to the bathroom and discovered me sitting at Mother's bedside (no longer much of a surprise, by the way), I shared with her the strange occurrence that led to my extremely early arrival. She asked what time the curtain rod fell. She was curious about the timing because she was making a trip to the bathroom around 3:15 or 3:30 a.m. and observed Mother turning her head, appearing to look at the empty chair by her bedside. My sister had stayed until around 2 a.m. Her roommate surmised that Mother had decided she wanted someone to fill that chair and "called" me to come join her! Interesting.

Mother started doing her breathing thing again. This time the gaps were gradually getting longer. That was nothing new. However this time, her extremities were also beginning to cool down. That was different. Plus, she had not really responded to me this morning. As I continued to check, she appeared to be getting cooler and cooler. This was indeed unusual. Her feet usually remained warm no matter how her breathing changed or didn't change. This was different. *This time, Mother, maybe you succeeded. You brought me to you in the still of the early morning hours. Smart lady. It's working.*

Then, from a peaceful place where we were both easing into another zone, we were instantly jerked back into the realities of nursing home life. The on-duty nurse (who happened to be the one who had been unknowingly disrespectful of my presence) flipped the overhead lights on and immediately started chattering. I quietly murmured, "Lousy timing." "How are you doing?" she asked. I know she hadn't realized I was there; nevertheless, it felt very intrusive. "I have to check on her," she explained. Well, there goes Mother's best effort so far.

She hadn't had any morphine all night, and this particular nurse didn't like to give it. So she had to wait till the day shift to get any medication. And then, because it still was "PRN" versus "scheduled," she had to wait until someone put it into their rounds . . .

Another disruptive thing about nursing home life: not only were there buzzers constantly resonating through the walls, but there were frequent random announcements over the loudspeaker. There was a wonderful moment when I had entered a meditative state, Mother was peaceful, and I even felt one of those rushes of chills throughout my body—and then a loud, football-announcer-like voice interrupted the quiet, announcing, "Would the owner of the green SUV please turn off their lights!" Thanks.

Mother had a special mattress on her bed, provided when hospice folks came to her aid. It was great. The intention was to prevent bed sores, as I understand. However, it was noisy, periodically inflating and deflating. When we desperately wanted uninterrupted quiet, I'd secretly turn it off for an hour or two. However, once all the noise began again outside her room, I'd turn it back on to counteract all the distracting hall noises.

The nurse's interruption was essentially my "final straw." I was exhausted. I did realize that. My own journey of a few days had turned into a much longer one. My supervisor had been amazingly supportive (after all, I am a grief counselor at a hospice!). My coworkers were wonderful. I had enough accumulated paid time off that I could take the extra days without penalty. But, as each new day came, I had to re-evaluate my staying. I believed I was getting signs that her transition was indeed imminent. I also began to believe that this experience was as much about my own need to learn about death and dying as it was her "simply" having a difficult time exiting. She was being my teacher.

I was learning so many things—about my mother, about myself in relation to my mother, about dying, about grief. Yes, Mother, you have again resumed the role of teacher in my life. Thank you. As the days progressed, I began to thank her. I also asked her if she minded if I wrote about this experience. I believe Mother actually enjoyed writing herself. After all, we were pen pals for many years. She had a quirky style of writing, as do I. Perhaps I was a newer, "improved" version of Mother without as much psychological/emotional baggage attached. It's a thought.

Mother began "arching" somewhat, almost as if she were having a sudden pain somewhere in her trunk. This was new and rather subtle. To me, it seemed to be an indicator of pain. I called the hospice nurse to inform her. She again affirmed my call. Yes, most definitely, arching is a sign of pain and discomfort. Again, that was confirmation that my being there was purposeful.

You see, I was getting conflicting messages from my family. We're all very different personalities. I am definitely looked at as the "oddball" a lot. I have a lot of weird (one of my favorite words!) ways of viewing the world, life, faith, spirituality, etc. Perhaps a different word would be "non-mainstream" or "alternative." Who knows? I just am who I am and no longer make any apologies for it. My worldview works for me, and for the most part, I consider myself relatively healthy overall (emotionally, mentally, spiritually). But there were conflicting views about my staying day after day after day. The general opinion was that I should go home to my own family. Each day I would reassess. I truly believed Mother had called me. I truly believed I was there to help her die. Every day she "chose" to stay around I began to look at it as a new lesson for me as well. I was learning—constantly.

And death and dying are not predictable. All kinds of variables interact with one another. There are physical, psychosocial, spiritual, family, and even environmental variables (the latter was a new one, added to my list while in the nursing home). I was continuing to learn. Who knows? Maybe there were/are inexplicable, cosmic forces at work, far beyond the limits of our awareness. The universe is so marvelously intricate, and God is so infinitely and ultimately present and all-knowing; how can we even begin to comprehend the mysteries that abound?

Chapter 20: The Hospice Room Brings a Preview of Heaven

Mother's hospice nurse had her own story of a family member's longer-than-expected dying. And the hospice social worker had a similar tale. Every day, their family members' signs had pointed to that being "their day to die." And it wasn't. There is no perfect prediction. I believe it is a combination of God's timing and ours. I'm not contending that we can circumvent divine timing. However, I believe that God's ultimate grace allows for the human need for growth and understanding. Sometimes the understanding does not come, however, until afterward. Looking back, we often are able to make sense of the timing. When we're in the middle of it, it can be very confusing.

Mother was someone who was always sensitive to environmental changes. Of course. We all are in our family, in one way or another. Just this morning, the toe of my sock didn't go into my shoe correctly. I had to redo it a couple of times before it was acceptable! Most of us have allergies. We're tuned in to the world around us. Perhaps we're overly tuned in at times. She was showing me that this can indeed play a factor in the dying process. She never had consistent quiet. She never even had the opportunity to be alone to take her final steps through the veil, if that were what she would choose. Plus, she didn't even have access to consistent medication. The hospice nurse was trying to get the doctor to schedule the morphine, but at this point, he was only willing to schedule it every eight hours. That wouldn't work—we were managing to get it about every five hours, which is better than eight! The last straw. Yes, the last straw. I was very frustrated.

I called my older sister to vent and to brainstorm. She suggested we ask about the hospice room again. Great idea! Since it wasn't available when it was first brought to our attention, I had not thought of it again. So I called the nurse and the social worker and left messages for both, inquiring if it would be available for us sometime soon. The social worker came by and told me she was beginning to work on it. The tricky part was that the patient had to be "actively dying" in order to be approved for the move. Also, once we moved her, she would be giving up the room she had had for almost four years . . . and her roommate.

That's fine! I was convinced she was dying, although I had been convinced since June.

Of course, hospice would not have approved her had they not been able to get a doctor to sign off on her having a prognosis of six months or less. So, I was not the first one to conclude that she was indeed dying. The timing was what was in question. I talked with the social worker and later with the nurse. The nurse said she had spoken in support of Mother being transferred to the hospice room. Yes, she said, all the signs pointed to the imminence of her passing. But they were the spiritual types of signs rather than the more traditional physiological signs of death's nearness. So, if she ended up living beyond a ten-day window, she'd have to be transferred back out of the hospice room. She would be able to stay in the nursing home, so that was not a concern. And her roommate was already processing her own grief (one of the issues we almost forgot to address, by the way!). She believed it would help Mother to have more quiet as well.

Out of the blue, the "movers" (perhaps the earthly equivalent to the "helpers"?) showed up to take Mother upstairs to the hospice room, and by one o'clock that afternoon, we were in "heaven on the fifth floor." The trip up there was actually rather fun. Mother had her eyes open as they wheeled her, in her hospital bed, out of her home of some years, down the hallway, through the middle of the dining hall (where some residents were still lingering after the noon meal), into the crowded elevator, and up to the fifth floor. Mother's eyes were almost excited with the adventure. She reached out her hand, just needing someone, anyone, to hold onto as she was rolled hither and yon.

Even as the elevator doors opened, I felt a greater sense of calm. The colors were muted, the lamps in the hallway were recessed. There was less commotion in the hallways, less noise. It was wonderfully peaceful. Later, when I inquired why her specific floor was first selected (particularly since she had been living on a more expensive floor!), my sister explained that it was the "renovated" floor. They had not yet gotten around to renovating the fifth floor. Mother's old floor was indeed brighter, more colorful, but that was a mixed blessing. At this point in her journey, the fifth floor was our heaven.

In the room itself, there were lovely decorations and no overhead lights. It was obviously a private room and felt even bigger than the double room she had shared with a roommate. Ahhh. And a quirky little surprise: there was a coffee machine, which furnished, at the push of a button, coffee—decaf or regular—and hot water for tea. Interesting. I now discovered that my dream itself was an affirmation of our decision to move to "heaven on the fifth floor." And having the social worker in the dream with me was further confirmation of this being the right decision, because she was the one who eventually was able to arrange our transfer. *Thank you, God. Thank you, Mother.* It was indeed all in divine order.

And outside the door was a sign that read, "Family hospice room." So now, instead of being in a mixed room, serving both the living and the dying, we were in a room that was clearly honoring the end of life. I quickly began using the lighting to our advantage. Even at night, whether I was curled up on the couch or in bed at my sister's, when any staff would enter the room, it was clear that we wanted the environment to be one of peace. It was a sacred space.

At times I would even play angelic music in the background. Sitting by Mother's bedside from that point on, it was a zone of peace, of transition. I would sit for hours, not even aware of my surroundings, almost in a bubble. If a full bladder got my attention and I had to rise up and walk to the restroom, I would suddenly discover I was tired. But once I reentered the zone, I would be fully present in the bubble, with Mother.

Chapter 21: Profound Reflection and Illumination

At times I would reflect on her face. There were moments when we switched places. I was the mother and she was my child. The bond was stronger in those moments than I could ever have imagined, crossing space and time, stretching across eternity.

I thought of how the essence of my creation was within her and that the essence of my own daughter's creation was within me. I pondered on reflections in a mirror. My maternal grandmother had a precious little vanity that had a central mirror and two movable mirrors attached on the sides. Each side could be turned inward. As a child, I enjoyed moving the side mirrors in such a way that the reflection would be a never-ending cascade of me! Reflection of reflection of reflection—infinity. It is as if our lives are never-ending reflections of one another. There's something amazing about the mother-daughter reflection—birth to birth to birth.

I was delighted when my daughter wanted to keep the vanity. It's now in her possession. She has inherited a love of tradition. Some, not all, of course. She is making her own.

Day 13. We're now in "heaven on the fifth floor." What a difference. Even the nurses have a more accepting orientation to end of life care. Awesome. I'm grateful. There's an interesting change, however, in Mother's overall condition. She no longer did her breathing thing. After she moved to "heaven," the intermittent breathing never returned. Never. That evening, I was able to leave with my own sense of peace. Synchronistically, on the way home, the only song I heard on the radio was, "We are family . . . I got all my sisters with me."

It's day 14, and we're still in "heaven." The sense of peace is wonderfully pervasive. Of course, the staff and residents are not as familiar as they had become on Mother's old floor, but the trade-off was somehow worth it. She had really calmed down. I had really calmed down. I'm sure there was a connection. Perhaps my restlessness had contributed to hers and vice versa. But, for now, we were both more at peace. Thank you, God. And thank you, nurses, for your openness to this part of our journey. We are grateful.

There were moments while in "heaven" that Mother would almost look like a small child at an amusement park, never tiring of one new adventure after another. I asked her, "Are you excited?" She nodded. I believe she knew she was about to embark on her own great adventure into a new world.

Sometime late that morning, during one of the seemingly thousands of times I was holding Mother's hand, standing at her bedside, she looked up into my eyes and said, "Don't leave . . . heaven." I couldn't understand precisely what was mumbled in between "leave" and "heaven," but my mind filled in her words to say, "Don't leave me till I'm in heaven," because she then said, sweetly, "Goodbye," and pursed her lips, inviting a kiss. I kissed her on her lips, she closed her eyes, and that was the last time she spoke.

She still continued to hold my hand. If I tried to pull away, she'd grab on with an amazing grip considering how weak she surely was due to the lack of food and water. Eventually, she relinquished her grip. I thanked her again for all the gifts she had blessed me with, including the joy of writing. I told her I was looking forward to writing about our experience together—she had inspired me in unimaginable ways.

Sadly, there were still some layers of consciousness remaining. She'd begun reflexively clenching her teeth even when the nurses administered the liquid morphine from a dropper. Although I'd warn each nurse, they each had their own confidence about administering the drug. "It won't be a problem," they'd boast, which would soon be followed by tugging on a dropper, trying to free it from Mother's literal "death grip." (Perhaps that's where the saying comes from!) Her teeth were clenched so tightly, she created a serious indentation on the dropper!

She also appeared to be experiencing new pain, this time whenever her leg was touched. Just as the nurses differed in temperament and attitude, so did the aides. There was quite a variety. A pair of aides came in to see if she needed changing. One leaned down and whispered in her ear, "Say hello to God for me . . . I need to talk with him . . ." She later shared with me, "I get the chills when there are angels present—they're all over this room. I felt it when I walked in." Then, directly to Mother, "Ann, you'll have your wings soon." She also added the thought that Father, Ann's husband, might be standing at the foot of the bed.

I hastened to say, "She has mentioned seeing her mother and daddy, but she hasn't mentioned Father, so we've stopped bringing him up. Theirs was not the smoothest of marriages."

Chapter 22: Letting Go Is Complicated

Day 15: I awoke to a lot of chills, even though the air temperature was very comfortable. The song in my head was, "Sure as the sunrise, I'll stand by your side. Sure as the daybreak, I'll love you for heaven's sake." I had promised her I'd stay "till heaven." This was the end of the second week I'd taken off from work. Little parts of me were beginning to get nervous about staying. There were definitely different opinions about my staying or going. Some believed I should have gone many days ago. However, each day, I renewed my willingness to be with her on this journey, regardless of the "opposing forces" (i.e., the rest of my family).

My daughter is a big dreamer herself. When we talked, she shared that she dreamed of lying beside Grandma. Nice. Grandma and my daughter were both strong-willed people at times; consequently, they sometimes "butted heads." One of my prayers of gratitude was that Mother had lived long enough for my daughter to see things from a more grown-up perspective, essentially letting go of any residual negative feelings about her grandmother. Her having a dream about her was a very positive sign for me. Thank you, God.

This was/is/will be an incredible journey for me. Was I being selfish about staying? I don't believe so. I can't be sure. Was there harm in my staying? I don't believe so. Did she need me to go in order for her to progress in the dying process? I don't know. At this point, I don't believe so. I honestly don't know. My "gut" belief is that this process would have been even slower had I not joined her in this journey. Is that "Truth"? Of course, I cannot say one way or another.

What was amazing was having one realization after another about how much she and I had in common! Mother loved to journal about her life. She would write things on random little scraps of paper. And I'm horrible about writing things down on scraps of paper, then carrying around this and that till it gets consolidated (or not!). I do believe she loved writing, although most of what I was privy to were her letters I was honored to receive. Her father liked to write poetry, and her mother was a sculptor and painter, so she had the creative genes, for sure.

Mother had begun to "dance," as I chose to call it, days before. She would hold her arm up in the air, as if in an embrace. It seemed to be with someone taller than she was. We tried asking her who her partner was, but just as she could not identify the "helpers," she didn't offer any hints as to the invisible tall person's identity. It was amazing how long she could hold her arm up in the air, poised so elegantly. Amazing. And, when her eyes were open, her gaze often shifted around the room as if she were watching others. She would reach out, as if waiting for others to reach back.

That early morning, we cuddled as the sun rose. In our heavenly room we were now able to observe the outside world when we chose, unlike in the room downstairs where her roommate had the window view. I took a picture as the sun crested over the tree line, a pink glow over a parking lot. She seemed present that morning, at least for a while. I asked if she were in pain. No. I asked if there were anything unfinished—anything she needed to convey to her children. Her eyes then drifted away again and her breathing became more shallow. I guess not.

Later in the morning, she was able to take sips of water. Water is a sacred symbol of life and its fluid nature. To share water with Mother in those last moments was as much a gift to me as it was to her.

By now she could only take water when it was dribbled from a straw. Her lips were parched and I would attempt to soften them with salve. She was slipping away incrementally. My care for her at this point was stroking—her cheek, her hand, her hair—stroking, gently stroking.

In trying to decipher what stones were left unturned, the only thing I could come up with was my brother. This time he had not come to see her. For most people, this might seem so incredibly obvious. However, since last time (in June) Mother had seemed so willing to let go before anyone else showed up, I suppose I thought she might do the same this time. Plus, we'd invited him by phone to at least remotely join the "party." However, since nothing else seemed to be urging her onward on this journey, I called my brother. Yes, they would come. They would be here in the morning. Wonderful!

Chapter 23: Stay or Go? Stay or Go? Stay or Go?

On day 16, Mother was still holding her own. However, she was definitely showing signs of distress, even moaning when she was turned or changed. I suggested we pre-medicate her before the diaper change; however, due to the constant turnover of staff (different shifts, different schedules, etc., very understandable), that message didn't stay consistent.

I said earlier that our exchange of words about "staying till . . . heaven" was her last verbal communication, which I interpreted as her wanting me to stay until she was gone. There still were occasional times when I asked if she wanted water and she'd surprise me with a "Yes, please," but those were few and far between.

That morning the hospice nurse on call for the weekend came by to check on Mother. She took her vital signs, observed her, then called me into the hall. She had been told I'd been "holding vigil" at the bedside for many days, extending my visit one day at a time, each day expecting death to be imminent. Today, she told me there were no signs at all pointing to her dying soon. I was hearing so many different messages, with my family wanting me to go home and the nursing home staff recommending I stay. And now, a hospice nurse was suggesting I go home. Again, my hesitation about leaving was two-fold. Not only had she "called" me to come, but she also had verbally asked me not to leave till she was in heaven. That's a difficult promise to break. But I would consider the nurse's advice, of course.

Later on that morning, my brother and his wife appeared. There were some lovely, warm moments, and some pictures . . . Many of us followed in our father's footsteps with a love of photography. Sadly, these pictures of Mother were more reflective of her impending death than of her full and active life.

Remember the birthday balloon? It was still flying; however, now it was flying at half mast. I used the E.T. analogy to relate my "heartlight" being turned on. I began looking at the balloon like the flower pot in the movie. In the movie, the flowers would flourish when E.T., the extra-terrestrial, was alive and well. As he was dying, the flowers began to wilt. I saw this as the balloon beginning to wilt.

Later that day I talked to Mother about how it was time for her to go be with her mother and daddy, just as it was time for me to be home with my family. It's time. It's time. I also reminded her that, when she leaves this time, to please turn off the switch, unplug, disconnect, shut down her body before she goes. I asked her to disconnect from the Power Source that kept her body running, recognizing we are never disconnected from the ultimate source of power—God. She is and always will be connected to God.

When I began speaking of her mother and daddy and how it was now time to be Home with them, she smiled and pursed her lips for me to kiss her once again.

My poor husband and daughter had been practically on call this whole time, riding the roller coaster with me, up and down, yes and no, she's dying, no, she's not. . . . My husband even went out and bought a suit, fully thinking he'd be racing up the highway to join me in full funeral regalia almost two weeks ago. And our daughter—despite any "history" she and Mother had—wanted (at minimum) to be with us as a support to me and my whole family. What a dear. But her life was now different from two weeks ago: a new semester was about to begin at college, so it would not be as easy for her to get away.

Later that evening, the lovely, compassionate nurse (I love this floor!) actually took me out of the room and sat me down, offering to help me decide what to do. He shared something I had never heard before. It was something he called the "3-3-3 rule." He said you can live three weeks without food, three days without water, and three minutes without oxygen. At this point, her last intake of anything food-like whatsoever had been two, maybe three days ago. She still got occasional dribbles of water, but not at all consistently. Nevertheless, he suggested I set a deadline and stick to it.

So again, I told Mother, "It's time for you to go Home to be with your family and for me to go home to be with mine." Big *H* for her, little *h* for me. But both very important.

I hung out with my brother and his wife for a while that evening, which was relaxing. I occasionally use a pendulum to help me get inside my own subconscious (that's one of the ways I interpret its seemingly involuntary movements) for yes and no answers to questions that are exceptionally difficult. So, I pulled out the pendulum to ask if it would be okay for me to go get a full night's sleep. "Yes," the pendulum answered! Thank you!

That night I decided someone would be traveling tomorrow. Either Mother would die tomorrow and my two family members would head this way, or Mother would still be hanging in there tomorrow and I would head home. It was time. I'd decided.

Chapter 24: I'm Leaving—Will She Go Too?

Day 17. In the morning, I packed my car. My intention was to leave that day! But before leaving my sister's house, I received a phone call from my friend, with whom I'd been consulting some during my stay with Mother. She said, "This will sound very strange, but, after it came to me, I let it 'sit' overnight before sharing it, to see if it still sounded right the next morning . . . and it does." She then described the image she had gotten of my father somehow interfering with Mother's passing. Okay, he's been gone how long? Some 26 years. Of course, my belief is that—in the spirit world, in heaven, on the Other Side, whatever you choose to call it—time doesn't matter. It's irrelevant. So Father could have just as easily died yesterday.

My friend shared that she believed Father still felt as if he had some ownership of Mother's body, and therefore he was fighting, from the Other Side, to keep her around in physical form somehow. I flashed on that Monday, when, intermittently, Mother's face had changed to an angry, mean face, and she said things like "Scat" or "Get out of here." Strangely, that would fit if she were being "held back" by another spirit. Perhaps I was here to encourage her to die (which was accurate, of course!). Very strange concept. Strange.

My friend then suggested that I enter Mother's presence as a healer instead of as a daughter that morning. Go in, first asking for divine protection, of course, but also declaring that only those whose intention is for Mother's highest good be allowed to enter. Then, ask for "helpers" like Jesus, Archangel Michael, Quan Yin, and any higher being who could, to assist in severing any lingering connection that Father (or any other being) might be trying to hold onto and which was keeping Mother from going on into the Light.

I'll try it! It can't hurt.

So, when I entered Mother's room that morning, I quietly did that. By midday, Mother truly was beginning the "active dying" process. I was noticing physical changes I had not seen before, as were others. The hospice nurse happened to drop by, perhaps trusting her instincts; and, sure enough, things were dramatically different. She said, "Today, she's totally different than she was yesterday."

When the aide came to change Mother, I helped turn her. Her body was now essentially lifeless. Even one of the nurses I had befriended gave me a hug, saying, "I know you'll be gone tomorrow." She believed Mother would be "gone," too.

It was a strange day in many ways. A massive storm front was moving through the city. Thunder was blasting loudly enough that we were frequently startled. Lightning was flashing as I walked through the halls toward the elevator with bags in hand. Then the lights went out. The emergency generators had to kick on to bring back the lights. Even the hallway doors that had never been closed starting automatically closing!

I kept walking toward the elevator. I even had my finger on the "down" button, then decided to make one last trip to say goodbye. After all, the brief journey I'd expected with Mother had turned into a very different adventure. I felt sure she was literally in the final stretches of her journey. I actually believed that her soul had already departed and that this was "simply" the physical part, shutting down the physical form which was no longer needed. That belief had allowed me to leave and not stay for her last breaths. As far as I was concerned, I had been there for the end. It just might not have been the last milliseconds of her life.

I walked back down the hallway one more time. The nurse who had tried to talk me into staying was nevertheless supportive of my leaving. One possible explanation for Mother still being around was that she had gotten used to my undivided attention (although I'd made many efforts to leave her alone, if that's what she wanted). I believed she finished. My hesitation was about leaving her alone. I'd come this far. My older sister called me, while I was in the room, to ask about a bottle of wine I'd left at the other sister's house. She asked, "Are you still there?" Hesitating, I replied, "Yes . . . it's just hard to leave her alone. She truly is actively dying now, and I've come this far—I just don't want her to have to die alone." My sister offered, "So, if I come, you'll leave?" "Absolutely." "Then I'll come." She also told me that I didn't have to wait for her—it would take her a little while before she could get her things together to get there. She encouraged me to go ahead and leave, trusting she would be there before too long.

I suppose she knew me well enough to realize I'd stay until someone showed up, so she sent her husband. I had written notes for whoever would follow me, describing some of the processes to which I'd become accustomed. I'd kept notes about when they'd given her morphine last, etc., and how often she was usually able to get it. I explained how she'd occasionally get sips of water, how she'd clench her teeth when they delivered the morphine through the dropper, etc. I was handing over this very special assignment to other, very capable people.

Fortunately, by that point, all the pieces of their extensive home remodeling had come to an appropriate stopping point, so they could help out more. I was ready to pass it on, ready to allow someone else to take the reins.

One more kiss goodbye.

Chapter 25: Time to Pass the Baton

By the time I got in my car and drove to the highway, I was convinced I had made the correct decision. She no longer needed me. And the others needed to share in this part of the journey. Divine timing once again. I drove through the storm to get home. That was tricky but manageable. I was on enough of an adrenalin "high" to stay awake. The events of the last few days were still reeling through my brain.

After about three hours on the road, I called my sister. I was thrilled when she explained that she had packed up lots of things to work on (she's very task-oriented) and was planning to spend the night in the hospice room with Mother. Hooray!

It was almost midnight when I pulled into our driveway. My husband greeted me warmly. I think he missed me! I was glad to be home.

I went back to work the next day, attempting to melt back into my life as a grief counselor. It was a surreal experience to "play normal" once again. I realized I was seeing things differently somehow. When I pulled into the parking lot of the doctors' building where I work, I noticed an acorn on the pavement, picked it up, felt it, looked at it (I'm probably lucky I didn't taste and smell it as well!), then put it in my pocket.

When I stepped into the elevator and looked at the letters and numbers by the buttons, I saw one with two *L*s—what is that? Why are there two *L*s? Where am I? At the nursing home, there was also a "double *L*" button. My senses were definitely still floating in that alternate reality!

I rode the elevator up to the fourth floor, got out, and started touching the walls. There is texture to the wallpaper! Was it there before? I don't recall. Even the color of the wallpaper looked different—a lovely, muted aqua. As I walked down the hallway to our office suite, I chuckled, secretly hoping there weren't hidden video cameras watching my every move!

At about 2 p.m., my sister called. There had been no change all night. The hospice aide had come in the late morning, and Mother seemed very uncomfortable being moved at all. She said that Mother's fingers and feet and knees had begun to turn bluish (as reported by the nurses). They were finally able to get morphine scheduled for every four hours plus PRN. It's about time! I also thought that, by now, it probably didn't really matter. She was basically gone.

When I called my sister that evening, she described a horrific day. As Mother's body was shutting down, there were very difficult things to witness (which, thankfully, don't occur very often). She had a lot of what our nurses call "terminal secretions." It took the hospice nurse plus two other nursing home nurses to get her adequately suctioned, etc., to eventually make her more comfortable. Fortunately, by the time my other sister arrived after her workday, Mother had settled down and was peaceful the rest of the night. My younger sister had been the closest to Mother emotionally. I don't believe she could have handled watching the physical challenges Mother's body was experiencing that day.

I talked with my older sister again the next morning. She said, "If things are as quiet today as they were last night, I'll be sleeping at home tonight." In fact, she stated, "Last night was boring!" (I guess so, after such a bad day!) Later that morning (around 10:30 a.m.), in the middle of a home care team meeting, I had the same *whoosh* of energy pass over me that I'd felt on the day I thought Mother had died. Since I had my phone with me, I sent a message to my sister (still in the hospice room, I presumed), saying, "Did something just happen? I had a very bizarre feeling hit me just now." She answered, simply, "No." Okay, I guess not, but it really felt like something had happened. (Maybe Mother just did another "fly-by"!)

It was still surreal being back in the so-called "normal world." Even typing on the computer, I realized I wasn't even thinking about spelling. I'm always persnickety about spelling. And capital letters? Are they really that necessary? My perception truly had changed. Would it be permanent? I didn't even consider it at the time, because it simply was what it was. I had no interest or concern about what might be. I had been in an alternate universe for 17 days.

I can't even imagine what it's like for people who are on a "death-watch" for years. I would imagine that what many may consider "abnormal" becomes normal. In working with grieving folks, I remind them that "normal" is a relative term and that everyone's grief is uniquely their own. There seem to be commonalities, for sure. But time frames and trajectories? There's no clear prediction of how long, how deep, etc. anyone will travel in the very real journey of grieving. Hopefully, there will be healing at some point down the road.

At some point. And change? Absolutely, the loss of someone
in your life will create change. That's inevitable.

Even with Mother's expected (and, to be honest, hoped for) death, I felt things that were a bit disorienting at times. Fortunately, because of the work I do and listening to story after story from people experiencing a very wide variety of losses, I knew that the one thing I could predict was that "it" would change . . . eventually. Growth and healing were things I was willing and eager to anticipate. Thank you, God!

That evening, I packed up my assorted bags and left the office to make my own journey home. As I approached the elevator, my phone rang. I fumbled to get it out without dropping anything. It was my sister. I answered, and she said, "I never asked you how you wanted to receive the news when Mother died. . . . Well, she died." Okay, I guess we don't have to discuss how I want to receive the news now, do we?!

There were no tears at that point. I had said goodbye many times during those 17 days, and even weeks before, when we went through our "dress rehearsal" as a family. I felt her "fly by" this morning, and believed that her soul had essentially vacated her body before I left. She was finally finished. And I was not sad; I was elated. Mother had graduated. She had graduated into the next plane of existence, into the Light. And I was pleased.

Years earlier, when Mother had informed me in a dream of her upcoming graduation, it was to be on something like the 11th day of the 11th month, at the 11th hour. Her official graduation was on the 18th day of the 8th month. Not quite as cosmically cool, but cool enough. With my attachment to numbers and the amazing beauty and depth of "sacred geometry," I'd been observing the numbers of the days all through this journey. I stayed with her 17 days at the end of her life. At some point in time, I realized I had been with her the first 17 years of my life. She died on a "1" day (numerologically, you add up all the numbers of the date, continuing until you get a single digit). It was the first day of the next phase of her Life. That's Life with a big *L*.

For the breathing of her last breath, my younger sister was with her. The two sisters had done the "changing of the guard." The older one, the chattier of the two, took long enough to leave the building that she was close by when Mother finally passed. Her last breath was peaceful. My sister simply looked up and noticed she was no longer breathing. Silent. Peaceful. She was gone. It was finished. This part of her journey was complete.

The next day, I had our usual Wednesday morning meeting with the grief support staff. For me it felt far from usual. Not only had I not been there the last two Wednesdays, but I'd been flying in an alternative universe for 17 days and counting. Fortunately, I was surrounded by caring, compassionate, trained grief counselors. When they asked how Mother was doing at the start of the meeting, I shared that she had died the previous evening. So, of course, they then asked how I was doing. I explained, as best I could, that I hadn't quite "landed" yet—the best description I could give them was that my plane was still circling the airport. When it would land, I wasn't sure.

A fascinating circumstance among the grief counselors: four others had lost their mothers in the last two years. We could form our own support group!

I was able to finish out the week at work. We went "home" (that's such a relative term, isn't it?) to St. Louis that Saturday and had time at the funeral home, greeting old friends, meeting new friends, remembering. . . . It was strange, staring at her lying in the casket. This person, this body, didn't look anything like Mother! This woman had a very stern face, very serious and almost critical. The Mother I'd been with for those 17 days reminded me of an earlier version of my mother, a happier version, more life-loving and giving. That's the one I'm choosing to remember, to treasure. I'm ready—now!—to let go of any negative images I may still hold somewhere, if anywhere. However, I feel and believe that anything negative I may have held in any of the cells in my body is forever gone. That was another unexpected gift of my time with Mother. Thank you, Mother, and thank you, God, for the opportunity to let it go!

On Sunday, there was a lovely funeral at both sisters' and Mother's home church. I had written a summary of Mother's (and our) life. How in the world do you summarize someone's life? The poem I wrote by her bedside was also included in the little program Mother's firstborn had created. She had asked me to read the poem as my contribution to the shared words and stories. I didn't expect to be fighting back tears. Of course, I did get teary. It was a very emotional time.

Chapter 26: Today We Bury Our Mother

That Monday morning I awoke to another dream. My husband's mother (who had died almost 12 years earlier) showed up! Would she be there—in heaven—to greet Mother? Mother had no earthly sisters, so I suppose my mother-in-law would do just fine. She announced, "I'll hug you in a minute." (Perhaps she was eagerly awaiting Mother's arrival!) Another flash of an image from a dream was a huge balloon. It was massive, filling the entire room. Someone was trying to push it aside to get around it. It was a fan-like shape, somewhat similar to the birthday balloon that stayed with Mother till the very end (my sister had taken a picture of the balloon after she died—it was conveniently sitting in a chair by her bedside). The balloon in the dream was an orangish color. Was that for my daughter, a student at UT, whose predominant color is orange? Nice touch, Mother—how creative you are!

I'll confess that I took my dream journal with me into the little bathroom at the hotel to write out the dream fragments I'd retained. I didn't want to lose it, but I had to head to the bathroom first thing! What was hysterical . . . are you ready for this? As I was sitting there writing, the toilet paper roll, which was on a spring-loaded rod, popped to the floor! I swear! Just like the spring-loaded curtain rod had popped off the morning Mother woke me up at 3:30 a.m. Mother, you most definitely have a sense of humor! Or perhaps she wanted to furnish more "proof" so that folks who hear her story have a better chance of actually believing some of these unbelievable things.

We all got dressed in our very traditional black, preparing to gather at the National Cemetery. Mother had served in the military, as had Father. She had chosen to be buried with him. Our daughter had never been to a military burial before. I had, of course, when my father was buried. That was 26 years ago, however, and I remembered very few details. And our relationship was different. I myself was different. I was now a mother and had lived with my own husband for 28 years. It all felt very different.

It was a crisp pre-autumn day, the blue sky hinting of cooler days to come. Our cars lined up along the narrow road beside the rows and rows of white markers dotting the lush green landscape. As we entered this sacred space, I noticed the entrance labeled "National Cemetery" on one side had "Peace" on the other. I noticed "Peace" right away. Mother would have liked that. What am I saying? She *likes* it. Present tense. Yes, she feels present. Very present.

As our cars began their gentle journey toward the permanent ceremonial site for military burials, the expanse of the contoured hillsides filled with row after row of white markers was striking. Those humble markers symbolized the years of military service and sacrifice by thousands of men and women. For what? I like to believe it has been for the pursuit of peace.

The flag-draped casket was tenderly withdrawn from the long black hearse. Uniformed military personnel carried her body, the outer shell she'd vacated merely a week ago, permanently housed in a box. (It's as close to a cardboard box as we could get, Mother, per your wishes!)

An assortment of family and friends gathered beneath the shelter. Fortunately, the clear blue sky and fluffy white clouds were still visible. I had a momentary flash of conversations we'd had about what critters and images we saw in the clouds on days like this. (Or was that my own daughter's and my musings I recalled?)

The formality and precision was oddly comforting and very proper. We all listened to the pastor's words and joined in the prayers. I didn't realize the Prayer of St. Francis of Assisi was a favorite of Mother's. It most definitely was a favorite of mine. "It is in dying that we come to live." How fitting—she was being buried a month after her 87th birthday.

We reached for each other's hands through the singing of "Amazing Grace, how sweet the sound . . ." A song so familiar—tears interrupt the words—a voice or two manage to carry through to the end. More voices rally with the words, "When we've been there ten thousand years," somehow symbolically holding on to the promise of the continuation of life.

There was an explosive series of shots discharged—three officers firing three rounds each. It was ear-shattering, yet impressively powerful. Following the gun salute, two officers slowly, carefully withdrew the American flag from the casket, then meticulously, gingerly folded it with impeccable precision. It was presented to a female officer, who in turn presented it to my sister, saying wonderful words which included, "On behalf of the President of the United States." She said thank you for Mother's service in the Coast Guard during World War II. As the number of World War II veterans being buried daily in this cemetery is decreasing, sadly the casualties of other foreign wars continue.

A moving ceremony. Thank you, Mother, for your service to our country and to us, your children. We learned so much of what we know from you. May we take the best of all of that and carry it forward—even for ten thousand years—as we extend kindness and generosity and humility and service to others. May it continue.

Someone had suggested we collect the bullet casings. My sister-in-law faithfully did so, sharing one with each of the kids and grandkids. An unexpected touchstone of remembrance.

"Touchstones" can be anything at all! I wouldn't have expected a bullet casing to be something I'd hang on to. But it was symbolic of an earlier part of Mother's life. She and I shared our love of owls, so I have inherited the remnants of her owl collection. I was even blessed with the gift of watching a family of owls be born and raised (till they were able to fly away)—another unexpected connection to Mother eight years before she died.

We all had to get back home to our jobs and schools, so we changed clothes at the cemetery and began our journeys back to our respective homes.

Chapter 27: A Few Post-Scripts Appeared

The synchronicity continued, however. Just two days later, we received an advertisement for a *Highlights* magazine subscription. We hadn't gotten one of those in years! It was another memory from childhood. Mother, to make some extra money when we were little, would gather us in the car with her and go door to door selling subscriptions.

And another: I happened to go to church the following Sunday, exactly one week after her funeral. That morning I woke up, saying to myself, "I am my mother and my mother is me." The scripture on the front of the bulletin for the service was "I am my beloved's and my beloved is mine" from the Song of Songs! One of the hymns sung and played on the cello that morning (a rare treat in the worship service) was "Jesu, Joy of Man's Desiring." It was one of Mother's favorites and was the postlude at her funeral. Mother's instrument was the cello (we had a little family quartet many, many years ago).

In the sermon, our pastor talked about what he called "sexy spirituality." He talked about how God doesn't want to be separated from us (like Father perhaps didn't want to be separated from Mother, still wanting to be connected on the physical plane). This also happened to be the fifth Sunday, which our Sunday school class uses to catch up on sharing what's going on in our lives. So, instead of feeling as if I were monopolizing the sharing, I was encouraged to share more of my story of the last several weeks.

And the gal I sat next to up in the balcony had lost her mother about a year earlier. We shed tears and hugged, comforting one another. I had encouraged her to speak with her family about hospice. It turned out to be a blessing to their family too.

Chapter 28: Gratitude and Humility

When Mother and I first connected through the ethers those many months before her death, I had no idea what was in store. Nor can I even begin to explain in any tangible way what transpired between us, two souls humbly traveling this earthly journey.

I believe we are placed on Earth with a purpose. In general I believe we are all ultimately here to serve the greater good of humankind. Discerning how that unfolds can indeed be a lifelong quest!

Each soul may, of course, have a multitude of "sub-purposes." I think one of mine is to walk with others as they traverse the often treacherous pathway from loss to healing. Loss may not always be the loss of a human they love. There are lots of different losses that are difficult to navigate.

This journey with Mother was one I could never have foretold, but it's one for which I'll be eternally grateful!

During those days I was with her at the end of her life, I was blessed with the space and time to reflect. Before that, I really hadn't paused long enough to ponder our relationship, our history, our connection, our life together and apart. We had so many things in common (including similar food sensitivities, large thumbs, exaggerated facial expressions, ridiculous-sounding squeals that appear out of nowhere . . .) that I hadn't taken the time to acknowledge, much less honor!

Allowing myself the space and time to be aware of and present with such marvelous details was delightful—and again, very unexpected. I am humbled that it took something as dramatic as impending death to draw those moments to me. I am now much more aware (even more than I was before this adventure!) of how precious and, yes, fleeting these moments can be.

I invite you to be more present, in the present, with those you love. We have them now. We have moments now to treasure. Please don't put off your enjoyment and recognition of those moments. Be present now. Be with yourself, be with others, now. That truly is all we have.

Thank you, Mother. And thank you, oh beloved Creator, Mother/Father God. What an amazing gift to be included in this eternal, sacred journey from our earthly home to our home in spirit. I am so grateful.

Chapter 29: Final Post Script—What I Wrote About This Very Special Child of God

This is the letter sent out the day of Mother's burial (via email—although Mother probably would have preferred a handwritten letter on a scrap of recycled paper!):

Dear Family and Friends:

Today, August 24, 2009, a month after Elizabeth Ann had her 87th birthday, we participated in a very moving ceremony at Jefferson Barracks National Cemetery. We watched in admiration as officers of the military, some from the Coast Guard (her branch of the service), fired nine rounds to salute her serving during World War II. They carefully folded the flag that had draped her casket, then handed it to my younger sister, who had been with her for her peaceful passing on Tuesday, August 18.

Mother leaves a legacy of faith, of laughter, of compassion, of delight in the world around us. I was privileged to be with her for 17 days at the end of her life. She was with me for 17 years at the beginning of my life, before I left home for college and then to Tennessee, where I began a new life and a new family with my own husband and daughter.

What an adventure to be with her those 17 days! It was an awakening for her and for me. I believe she was fully present for many of those moments together. She had been "absent" for many months, due to the cumulative effect of TIAs (mini-strokes). While sitting with her, observing her, listening to her, she taught me a lot about dying. She also allowed me time to reflect a lot on living. Those many days by her bedside were spent in a zone where time stood still. It altered or at least expanded my perception. (And for those of you who know me, my perception was already a bit "altered"!)

I believe we all truly are connected—one to another, to the Earth, to our Creator. Time and space are our creations to manage our earthly journey, however brief. I believe Mother gave me one last "parting gift" those last days due to my current position with a Nashville agency. For some synchronistic reason, I am currently a grief counselor with Alive Hospice, a marvelous not-for-profit agency in Nashville and the surrounding counties. I undoubtedly will be able to draw from my experiences these last few months in working with the individuals I serve. I believe I also will write about this journey.

I send this to each of you, knowing in the deepest parts of my heart that you too have been on a similar journey or have stood beside others in their journey. Each one of us will inevitably experience loss in our lifetime—it's simply and profoundly part of the human experience. So, I also share a poem I wrote as I sat at her bedside. Perhaps you can add your own "Signs of Life" as you read it, remembering precious times in this marvelous life we share.

Sending love and blessings to each of you, in gratitude for the loving thoughts and prayers directed our way in these recent days and months,

Ruth

This is the poem I composed while at her bedside during those last days:

Signs of Life

Signs of Life are found in the giggles of children
playing on a squeaky metal swingset.

Signs of Life are discovered in delectable mouth-freezing
snow cream
freshly created by devoted hands.

Signs of Life are heard in words written about a bear named
Winnie the Pooh
as we drift off to sleep.

Signs of Life are seen in imaginative creations
woven, sewn, or knitted by tender hands.

Signs of Life are experienced every day in simple ways,
too easily overlooked or forgotten.

As the body begins its deathward journey,
signs of life become a glance, a smile, or a gentle squeeze
of a hand . . . a word or two . . . all gifts.

Signs of Life become the rise and fall of the chest
as it continues to reach for fleeting moments of this life.

As Signs of Life in the earthly body begin to fade . . .
moment by moment . . . and then . . . vanish . . .

We pray for Signs of the next Life—
in a dream, a whisper, a nudge, or a tingle of recognition,
an honored presence of Spirit.

Signs of Life are precious—in any form, at any time . . .
all reminders of the fleeting and yet eternal nature of Life.

(For Mother, from Ruth, 8-18-09)

This is what I wrote that was included in the bulletin for her service at the church:

Elizabeth Ann

July 24, 1922—August 18, 2009

Ann was born on July 24, 1922. She grew up in Missouri, graduating from high school in 1940. She served with the Coast Guard, where she began her career with the federal government. She married Tom in 1947. They had four children, two of whom were born in Columbia while she and Tom were students at the University of Missouri. Ann got a bachelor's degree in home economics plus a couple of little girls as well.

They moved a lot while the girls were young, adding two more children to the picture just one year apart, when living in a tiny little town.

Life in their household wasn't boring. There were many adventures, as the little family moved all over the state of Missouri. Ann maintained her homemaker status until 1963, when she resumed her career with the federal government.

Even while the kids were still young, they went on some adventures. As the children got older, the adventures broadened and eventually included travel to places like the Galapagos Islands, Baja California (whale-watching), and Europe. They even made a cross-country trip to Alaska in a camper. Another exciting activity Ann engaged in was motorcycle-riding—she and Tom went on many trips together—sometimes on her own motorcycle.

Tom died of cancer in 1983; however, Ann still continued her exploration of other countries and cultures like China and Iceland.

Her life of adventure was also well-filled with time with family. She welcomed a couple of sons-in-law and a daughter-in-law into the family and eventually two grandsons and a granddaughter. Family gatherings were frequently filled with laughter, sometimes to the point of tears.

Today, amidst tears and laughter once again, we gather to honor Ann—mother, grandmother, and friend. Her life on Earth was well-lived and her death was a peaceful transition into the life to come. We love her and we will miss her. We are grateful we were in one another's lives.

* * * * * * * * * * * * * * * * *

Thank you, Mother, for all you have taught me—your deep faith in God, your love of nature and creation, your love of the written and spoken word, your love of beauty, your passion for service, and your love of family and friends. I'm so grateful to have been your daughter and am grateful that you continue to want to be connected.

Chapter 30: Post Script to the Post Script

I had considered calling this an epilogue. However, knowing that I don't always read epilogues myself, I'll call it the actual final chapter and hope you readers will do me the honor of reading it to discover why it took me so long to tell Mother's story.

I began writing this in 2009, within months of my mother's death. As I shared, I believe she was being my teacher in those last days. I was her humble and willing student, but primarily a grateful daughter.

It took me this long to finish the story because lots of life happened in the meantime.

My life has changed in many ways since the summer of 2009. I have moved to a new part of town, leaving behind a long-time residence and marriage, re-creating and re-discovering myself in some ways, and hopefully deepening the parts of me I continue to embrace.

I have felt Mother's presence off and on since her death. Call it a hunch, but I believe Mother has been one of my guides or so-called guardian angels throughout some of these changes in my life. This most recent leg of my journey has continued to be filled with synchronistic happenings! Life is difficult. Transitions and transformations often take leaps of faith and bursts of courage.

Being held in the invisible arms of those you love somehow makes it more tolerable. Just this morning I was blessed with another dream of Mother. The image was of her preparing one of her signature cherry pies. She wore one of Grandmother's embroidered aprons and was smiling. I still feel her support and love.

One of my major motivations for writing this book was to support having more conversations about death and dying and grief. And in our conversations, we need to share *all* of our experiences, including those that defy tangible explanations.

Death is part of life. It just is. And the magical, mystical presence of spirit deserves to be shared in more than shy whispers, behind closed doors. The more we share our stories with one another, the more we are able to encourage others to feel comfortable talking about their own experiences. Perhaps the more we speak freely, the more experiences will be provided for us.

This is one story—my account of returning to my hometown to be with my mother in the last days of her life on Earth. She was making her way to her own original home, where she was created by her own divine Mother. Full circle. Life's circle. Beginnings, endings, transformations, completions, initiations. But somehow still a circle, continuing ever-fluid and evolving.

I felt indescribable love in those last days. And it was not as if I'd been lacking in love or that I'd been yearning for a closer relationship with Mother. It was a lovely, unexpected gift. A return to Mother.

I believe it was orchestrated by some divine conductor, arranged to be played out as it was. Not precisely, because I believe completely in free will. But her spirit reached out to mine and our hearts were again connected. We somehow made our way those last days—teacher, student, mother, daughter, sister, friend.

My return to my own mother was only part of our journey in those days. At times I felt something so profound that I felt connected to the Divine Mother, the feminine aspect of God. And, as Mother was returning to her home from which she came, I also was returning home. I felt more at home than I had in years—connected to my family, my community of friends, my colleagues, and my sense of being at home in all those places, with all those people.

It all somehow melted together into a miraculous sense of wholeness, of Oneness. Mind, body, and spirit—beautifully interconnected. And connected to another dimension, another layer/level of existence that I believe is as real as anything else.

Before this amazing time with Mother, I already believed that we are all connected. This belief is now even more firmly a part of my very being. And I already believed that our essence—our spirit—does not cease to exist when the physical body dies. That belief now resonates with every breath I am granted and gratefully receive.

My hope for each of you:
May you enjoy the love and compassion of others.
May you find moments of joy to treasure every day you're given.
May you find the path that guides you Homeward.

Please note: Grief is real, and yet it's different for everyone. Many have a very natural resilience. A strong support system is a wonderful safety net, if you're blessed to have friends, family, a faith community, or other sources of support. If you have any questions, don't hesitate to at least check with a local hospice. Even if your loss had no connection to a hospice, many have trained professionals who can help you process what you are experiencing.

May you find comfort, healing, and peace.

Cover Photo Information

The cover photo is of a favorite piece of furniture, described in Chapter Twenty-One: Profound Reflection and Illumination. It originally belonged to my maternal grandmother. It's a charming vanity with movable side mirrors. I felt that it would be the perfect setting for the cover photo.

I was thrilled when my daughter wanted the vanity for her bedroom when it was time for Grandmother's furniture to be dispersed. My daughter has moved it many times, but it now has landed in the home where she's planning to begin a family of her own.

Just as we little girls stood and maneuvered the mirrors to reflect our own images multiple times, I attempted to position the mirrors to reflect the candle and its flame. To add some extra symbolism, I placed some of my mother's costume jewelry at the base of the candle holder, which sits atop the jewelry box my daughter has had since she was a little girl (some of you know it—the one with the ballerina!).

Four generations of women, and the love they share, are "reflected" in this photo.

Author Information

Ruth R. Williams, LCSW, lives in the Nashville, TN area and is thriving in this next chapter of life. She is passionate in her approach to life, which is expressed in her work as a grief counselor as well as in creative pursuits like music and photography.

Ruth is available for speaking and seminars for your business, organization, or faith community. Her first book, *The Prescription for Joy: How to Transform Yourself from Overwhelmed to Overjoyed*, is available through her website. She also has a CD of some of her original music (*New People for a New World*) and a meditation/relaxation CD (*Meditation of Joy*). For contact information or to order any of these products, please visit her website, ruthwilliams.com.

Made in the USA
Charleston, SC
27 June 2016